SILENT
CAPITULATIONS

SILENT CAPITULATIONS

✦

THE KEMALIST REPUBLIC UNDER ASSAULT

SEDAT SAMI

iUniverse, Inc.

New York Lincoln Shanghai

Silent Capitulations
The Kemalist Republic Under Assault

Copyright © 2006 by Sedat Sami

iUniverse books may be ordered through booksellers or by contacting:

iUniverse
2021 Pine Lake Road, Suite 100
Lincoln, NE 68512
www.iuniverse.com
1-800-Authors (1-800-288-4677)

ISBN-13: 978-0-595-38716-8 (pbk)
ISBN-13: 978-0-595-83174-6 (cloth)
ISBN-13: 978-0-595-83097-8 (ebk)
ISBN-10: 0-595-38716-0 (pbk)
ISBN-10: 0-595-83174-5 (cloth)
ISBN-10: 0-595-83097-8 (ebk)

Printed in the United States of America

To the memory of a beloved brother,
a genuine Kemalist

Ömer Sami Coşar

CONTENTS

PREFACE

On the eve of the greatest calamity to visit upon the nation, a little known Anatolian newspaper asked a profound question:

> While the fallen
> guard this land with eyes wide open,
> How honorable is it
> to go on living with eyes wide shut?

> —*Doğrusöz*, June 5, 1919

The idea of writing this book came to me while reading these lines.

The events of the past few years are a series of fire alarms, a response to which is now in order. The enemies of the secular republic are making a final push to prepare the ground for the arrival of the Islamic republic a.k.a. "the second republic."

Suffering from the ravages of tribal conformity and feudal customs, tainted by cronyism and religious fanaticism, the society is sleepwalking towards a Sharia state. When corruption has metastasized within the body politics, social justice rings hollow, corporations are controlled by a web of vested interests, and people with neither shame nor conscience rob the nation's patrimony and destroy its social and economic fabric, it is fair to say that the future of the nation is cloudy.

However, "sadder and graver than all these circumstances, those who hold power within the country" appear to have identified their party's interest with the political designs of international lobbies.

Therefore I feel, somehow, obligated to add my voice to those of all the others who, over the years, have fought against the betrayal of the Kemalist Revolution by successive generations of ruling elites, collaborationist intellectuals, corrupt businessmen, and feudal lords—all part and parcel of a system masquerading as a functioning democracy. Personally, the motivation to write this book was a very simple one: I owe too much to the republic in which I grew up—to the schools in which I was educated and trained, to the armed forces in which I served, and to the heartland in which I worked.

But there is an even more urgent need: to educate adequately and inform accurately the international public opinion about the seriousness of Turkey's slide into the abyss. It is imperative to demonstrate to readers, through a string of arguments and events, that Turkey can become a desirable, contributing, and respected member of the world community only after she has reached a high level of contemporary civilization and that this requires the adoption and the rigorous enforcement of the unfinished chapters of the Kemalist agenda.

Everything reported in this book has been in the public domain. Some are fresh and others are a few years old. They may not have been reported by the foreign media, but that is not unusual. In fact, when it comes to reporting about Turkey, the international media's attention span is very short. Topics which will command the most interest are national disasters, fiscal/financial crises, or terrorist attacks, especially those where some tourists have lost their lives.

An in depth analysis of Turkey's social, economic and political problems will rarely see the daylight. Such articles are careful not to offend the ruling power centers, especially when Turkey is viewed, by international investors, as an "emerging market" ripe for lucrative returns.

In the course of the two years that it took to put this book together, I have become forever indebted to very many people. To the courageous men and women of the Turkish media who reported the good, the bad and the ugly without discrimination, to the nationalist, the collaborationist, the socialist, the religious fanatic, the capitalist, and even to Karen Fogg's claque—you were my true eyes and ears, and I thank you for that! To friends and colleagues all throughout Turkey, I am most grateful. To the common folks of this beautiful land, from the cook aboard the gullet to the shoeshine boy in Erenköy, from the taxi cab driver hailing from Deliorman of Bulgaria to each and everyone with whom I have come in contact and who has given me cause to be upbeat, my heartfelt thanks. And a most special word of gratitude to E. for her comments, suggestions and corrections.

Last but not least: this book would not have been possible without the dedication and tireless efforts of the staff of iUniverse Publishers. A special word of gratitude to Jon McWilliams for supervising the project from end to end and to David Bernardi whose editorial comments were invaluable. However, the responsibility for the absence of footnotes and the non-conventional format under which the citations are given is mine.

PROLOGUE

○ ○

Nations who make a habit of looking for a way to earn their living without study and hard work are condemned to lose first their honor, then their freedom, and eventually their future.

—*M. Kemal Atatürk*

This is the story of a couple of very fateful years…

July 1, 2004

It has been twenty months since the November 2002 general election, which brought Recep Tayyip Erdoğan's (RTE) Justice and Development Party (AKP) to power in a landslide. Having cast about 34 percent of the votes, the Islamists controlled 66 percent of the seats in Parliament, thanks to an election law designed with one goal in mind: keeping fringe parties, including the political wing of the PKK, the terrorist/separatist Kurdish movement active mainly in the southeast, from being represented in Parliament. Ironically, by setting the minimum necessary for representation at 10 percent of the total national vote, Parliament had managed to bar more than the PKK. In fact, nearly half of all votes cast were for parties who would not be represented in Parliament.

Six months later, during the municipal elections of April 2003, the AKP won an even more impressive victory. On the surface, it appeared that the Prime Minister's (PM) honeymoon with the nation was headed for even better days. So when, during the NATO Summit held in Istanbul, M. Ali Kışlalı, a well-respected columnist for the Istanbul daily *Radikal*, published, without comments, the following mysterious poem, the public had to take notice:

Tear down my statues...

My fellow citizens
I am Mustafa Kemal...
If old fashioned have become
my ideas,
If science is still deemed
not the true spiritual guide,
Let me keep my mouth shut and
beg forgiveness...
Then forget all that I've said and
tear down the statues,
to honor me, you have erected.

If freedom is still not
the highest virtue...
If you approve
that slaves should remain in chains...
Then forget all that I've said and
tear down the statues,
to honor me, you have erected.

If contemporary civilization
has no meaning,
If the middle ages
are where you wish to belong,
If you can venerate
someone who spits unto the arts...
Then forget all that I've said and
tear down the statues,
to honor me, you had erected.

If not enough pain
was caused through violence and war,
If it is meaningless to preach
peace at home, peace in the world,
If there is a reward
for arms race…
Then forget all that I've said and
tear down the statues,
to honor me, you had erected.

If you are still longing
to wear fez or veil, and
prefer the dark of night
to the bright day's light…
If you still expect help
from sheikh or dervish…
If you seek healing from
amulets and sorcerers…
Then forget all that I've said and
tear down the statues,
to honor me, you had erected.

If, fearing the wrath of fanatics,
you deny a woman equal place to a man and
insist that she covers herself with a black cloth…
If you believe that it is fate that causes
our women and daughters to be illiterate…
Then forget all that I've said and
tear down the statues,
to honor me, you had erected.

If Liberty and Republic
have become too burdensome for you…
If you long for the days
of Empire and Sultan…
If you still have failed to grasp
the meaning of being a nation…
Then become servants, follow your congregation,
wait for the fatwa of the Sheik-of-Islam,
forget all that I've said and
tear down the statues,
to honor me, you had erected.
JUST LEAVE ME ALONE…

—Y. Apaydın

Kışlalı, who suspected the name Y. Apaydın to be a pseudonym, reported that the poem which was duplicated and handed out between friends and relatives had generated quite a stir in Ankara, the nation's capital. Its rather indignant tone reflected what many serious students of the political scene had already detected: The Justice and Development Party were gradually moving away from the Kemalist reforms of the past eighty years. Was Turkey faced with the early signs of a "second Republic?" What was the pulse of the nation? Had the "new and improved" Islamists failed to keep the promises they had made two years earlier, during the campaign leading to the 2002 general elections?

◆   ◆   ◆

In the summer of 2004, the Turkish media reported several events that, when contemplated as part of a mosaic, indicate the "state of the nation" at that time.

In Izmir, the metropolis on the Aegean coast, Mayor Priştina died suddenly at the age of fifty-two following a massive heart attack. An entire city—its buildings, busses, boats, and monuments—were all draped with the photos of the late mayor. A crowd estimated in excess of one million attended his funeral. What was the reason behind the affection of the people for this son of Albanian immigrants? First, as a mayor, he had done something quite unusual for a politician: he had delivered on his promises. Second, he displayed an even more unusual characteristic: he was honest. Could this be an indication of a profound longing and the symptom of a serious disease within the Turkish body politics? Three events that took place almost simultaneously in three different corners of Turkey may provide some clues.

In Istanbul, Prime Minister Recep Tayyip Erdoğan's eldest daughter got married while a king (of Jordan), a president (of Pakistan), and three prime ministers (of Greece, Italy, and Albania) stood as witnesses and seven thousand invited guests—most, if not all, covered from head to toe—sweated in the scorching July heat. Even though a NATO summit was also taking place at about the same time in Istanbul, the elite of the Islamic establishment was the main focus of the media's attention.

The wedding provided the public with a glimpse into the practice, among the wealthy members of the Islamic business establishment, of offering lavish gifts to the sons and daughters of the powerful. Indeed, RTE, when explicating his sudden acquisition of a significant fortune during his tenure as mayor of Istanbul, maintained that he had borrowed from his son, who in turn claimed to have made his fortune thanks to the generous gifts—in cash and gold—he had received at his wedding. No one was about to remind the guests of the various charges leveled against the former mayor of Istanbul prior to the general elections, which included official misconduct, embezzlement of public funds, the acceptance of bribes, and corruption during the awarding of public contracts. Following the elections all charges were dismissed for lack of evidence. Oddly enough, the prosecutor refused to appeal the verdict.

In another case, where similar charges were brought against the former mayor, he was found not guilty, and the new prosecutor failed to appeal that verdict as well. Surely, the fact that all these good judges and prosecutors were promoted to bigger and better posts, a few years after they have cleared the leader of AKP, must have been sheer coincidence.

At the other end of Turkey, near the Iranian border in the Province of Van, a rather sinister series of events were unfolding. The son of a prominent local tribal chief (Şerefhan tribe) was arrested in a nearby province while trying to sell opium to undercover policemen. The provincial authorities drove the suspect to an agreed-upon location, where he was to be turned over to law enforcement officials from Van, but the station was surrounded by armed members of the tribe who wrested the chief's son away from the hands of the police. He surrendered several weeks later after spending time in Iran.

Such a story may have deserved a modest place among the police pages of the local papers, but in the context of a society where tribalism is still dominant, the picture reflects something far more profound: the role of drugs in the economy of the region. And it is symptomatic of a society in the grips of violence, corruption and lawlessness.

The Province of Van lies along the transshipment route of all sorts of drugs originating in either the "Golden Triangle" (Laos, Thailand, and Burma) or the "Golden Crescent" (Afghanistan, Pakistan, and Iran). Even though it is an economically depressed region with an average per capita income well below one thousand dollars, all signs point to the injection into the region's economy of vast amounts of money of questionable origin. Luxury cars, especially brands such as Jeep and Mercedes, are familiar sights in downtown Van. Those who can afford it prefer to have big city license plates. During stop-and-search operations, vehicles registered in Van (license numbers beginning with 65) are searched far more thoroughly than cars with out-of-province license plates. Luxury shopping malls and villas are being built even though many remain vacant. Signs of conspicuous consumption suggest that Van has become a major center for drug money laundering. The events surrounding the arrest of the son of the tribal chief point also to the penetration of law enforcement by moles serving the tribe, the drug lords, and criminal gangs.

Finally, in Ankara, four members of parliament (MP) from the opposition Republican People's Party (CHP) resigned and joined the AKP, enabling the party to secure the requisite super majority needed in order to revise the constitution without resorting to a public referendum. What surprised many observers were that one of the four MPs was considered a strong supporter of the Kemalist reforms. On issues as diverse as the headscarf, religious schools, or Christian missionaries and Armenian propaganda, he was eager to submit questions to the relevant Ministers.

But he was a businessman too. Borrowing a page from Putin's Russia, the treasury inspectors had descended on his company headquarters, checking his tax returns and confiscating his books and computers. In the span of two short weeks, the man who had complained of a lack of Kemalist and reformist ideas in government was now joining the very gang who desired nothing more than to undo most of Atatürk's revolutionary reforms. While watching the Prime Minister smile and happily pin his party's emblem on the lapels of his new recruits, it was difficult not to remember the 2002 elections, when the candidate had pledged a transparent and clean government.

◆　◆　◆

In May 2005, one of the same MPs was expelled from the Party, after being charged with fraud. According to newspapers reports, the payback for joining to AKP may have been the award of a subcontract for the construction of a segment of the Baku-Tiflis-Ceyhan oil pipeline.

Even though corruption seems to be rampant throughout various segments of Turkish society, religious fanaticism and zealotry may prove to be the greatest danger facing the future of the secular republic. During demonstrations in Ankara (protesting the oppression taking place in Uzbekistan), the speeches at one open-air meeting quickly degenerated into a plea for the return of the Sharia in Turkey. The crowd carried banners with slogans like "True salvation, the Caliphate" and "Caliphate will be restored, despots will be tried" and held up signs indicating their support for the fundamentalist Islamic organization Hizb-ul-Tahrir. The demonstrators, calling the uprising an "Uzbek Intifadah" and accusing Islam Kerimov of colluding with the Jews, rejected the notion of a "Turkish nation" and called upon the "Ummah" or "Ümmet" (the nation of Islam) to rally around their caliphate state.

May 2005 is also the month when the Islamist majority in Parliament achieved one of the party's long-sought goals. In a series of amendments to the Turkish penal code, they voted to facilitate the establishment of unlicensed (i.e., illegal) Koran courses (a modern-day *madrasa*) in all sorts of locations where young children would be taught to memorize the Koran and would at the same time be indoctrinated into a lifelong commitment of supporting the goal of a Sharia state.

A battle for the hearts and minds of future generations is gaining steam. While the issue of Koran courses was debated in Parliament, the Ministry of National Education was reviewing proposals for all four years of high school curricula, including detailed topical outlines (course syllabi) for courses dealing with religion. Among the novelties proposed for the fall 2005 semester were visits to a mosque, so students could learn the ritual of ablution in a hands-on fashion. Special emphasis was also to be given to the reading of the Koran during the week when the faithful celebrate the birth of the Prophet Mohammed. Classroom demonstrations of the ritual of prayer, the showing of *The Call* (a made-in-Hollywood movie), and videos highlighting the pilgrimage to Mecca have been proposed as part of the new curriculum.

And yet nothing that took place during the past few years should have surprised a student of the Turkish political scene. Turkey is still not reconciled with her secular credentials. This is the fault of a large and corrupt force within the political establishment which, during most of the last half-century—in cahoots with a corrupt business community—appealed to voters by resorting to the most naked form of populism: the promise of, so-called, religious freedom! Every attempt by the left to shift the debate to the development of programs for the welfare of the masses was thwarted by an anti-secular right, which promised more of the same.

Prime Minister Erdoğan is caught between his desire to bring Islam, patiently but surely, to the forefront of Turkish daily life and his desperate need to placate the volatile secular republican forces. He hopes to achieve this by taking Turkey into the European Union (EU). However, all available evidence suggests that the present government is unable to accept unequivocally the secular nature of the Turkish state. Decisions and actions are taken not because they are in the best interest of Turkey's progress towards a civil society, within which men and women would be equally emancipated partners, but rather because they are necessary in order for Turkey to join the EU.

Unfortunately for the Prime Minister, nowadays the EU is not the only partner with whom Turkey has to deal. Turkey's financial and economic woes make it impossible for the Erdoğan regime to tackle them with courage and determination and without surrendering the control over the country's budgetary policy to the International Monetary Fund (IMF) and the World Bank. In the past, Kemalists always took pride in emphasizing the idea that "sovereignty belongs unequivocally to the Nation!" Today, that statement sounds hollow.

◆   ◆   ◆

One of the major promoters of Turkey's entry into the EU has been the nation's business community. Over the years, the Turkish business elite have established strong ties with their international partners. And during the same period, with the acquiescence of the political establishment, scores of private banks mushroomed. They collected massive amounts of deposits, all fully insured by the state, and siphoned them off into private businesses through questionable loans and investments. Most of this plundered national wealth later ended up tucked away in offshore accounts. The total estimated loss to the treasury is about $60 to $80 billion.

Rampant corruption at all levels of the Turkish society—but especially among the political establishment, the media, and the business community, with tax evasion among professionals and businesses reaching shameful levels—contributed to successive financial crises that further deepened the crushing weight of the national debt. Today, the country's total debt is approaching $250 billion, $20 billion of which belongs to IMF alone. The service on the public debt consumes almost 50 percent of the annual budget, leaving very little for health (3 percent), education (10 percent), and defense (4 percent). Having surrendered the control of the national budget to the demands of the International Monetary Fund and foreign creditors and unable to invest in job-creating infrastructure projects, Turkey's official unemployment rate jumped, over the last four years, from 6 to 11.2 percent, although the unofficial figure is probably closer to 22 percent.

The plight of those who were hoodwinked in Germany is another sad story. Appealing to religious sensitivities—Koran's admonishment against payment of interest—with the promise of financial rewards, without having to call it "interest," many so-called "green" holding companies siphoned off about 15 billions euros worth of savings from Turkish workers living in Germany. Many have lost their life's savings, while others have become paupers thanks to unscrupulous portfolio managers who have funneled the misappropriated funds to religious/ pious foundations.

◆   ◆   ◆

On a sunny summer evening (July 12, 2005), in a fancy Istanbul Hotel an unusual wedding was taking place. It was unusual, indeed, to see $15,000 worth of gold bracelets and $10,000 worth of pearls hung on a bride's arms and neck! The bride, the daughter of the 30,000-strong Karakeçi tribe's chief, was wedded to the son of the chief of the 45,000-strong Şaddat tribe. The cost of the wedding was estimated at $80,000, not counting the hundred dollar bills that were floating in the air (*Milliyet*, 7/13/2005). It was strange, indeed, to see two southeastern tribal chiefs flouting their wealth in such a conspicuous, almost obscene, manner, while thousands of members of their tribes were condemned to a life of poverty and hunger.

◆   ◆   ◆

"Istiklal caddesi" is a long, winding, colorful, and very busy boulevard at the heart of what used to be called Pera. Late at night, business establishments would place their trash bags for collection along the quaint and picturesque tramway line. Pedestrians walking along the line would get a certain whiff in the air which, up until now, I have always assumed to be caused by the presence of trash. But on a hot summer night in July 2005, the thought occurred to me that maybe, just maybe, the smell was none other than the decaying soul of a rotten and corrupt social edifice

1

A REVOLUTION
IN REVERSE GEAR

To listen to some European Union parliamentarians or to read some of the comments offered by media talking heads in Europe—and especially in Turkey—one might conclude that Kemalism is a dirty word. I am reminded of the distorted meaning the word "liberal" has gained in the United States. Yet the Kemalist Revolution had one simple goal: to elevate Turkish society to the level of contemporary civilization. In order to achieve this it proposed the development of a modern educational model, the elevation of women to equal status with men, and the separation of religious and state-related activities ("laicization" or secularism).

The foundations of secularism in Turkey were laid about a year after the declaration of the republic. In a speech delivered before the parliamentarians of his Republican People's Party, Mustafa Kemal gave the first signal of a long and remarkable journey: "Islam, of which I am a proud adherent, must be liberated from all politics that has ensnared it for centuries, and the law of the land must be purged from rules based on hollow principles." On another occasion, he said, "Read our history, listen well, and you will discover that the ills that enslaved and ruined our people have always been the results of abhorant acts appearing in the guise of religion."

Following the convening of Parliament on April 23, 1920, the adoption of a constitution on January 20, 1921, and the end of the sultanate, the republic was declared on October 29, 1923. The following year, a succession of laws established the inexorable march of the revolution: the removal of all religious symbols from the classrooms, the unification of education, and the closure of Sharia courts. Then, on February 25, 1925, it became illegal to use religion for political purposes. All dervish convents and all places serving religious recluses were closed. In 1927, courses on religious topics as well as Arabic and Persian language

11

courses were removed from the secondary education curriculum. The following year, instruction in all high schools became co-educational. During the same year (1928), Article 2 of the constitution was amended and the statement "The religion of the Turkish State is Islam" was deleted. The oath taken by the parliamentarians no longer referred to "Allah" but rather to the "honor" of the person taking the oath. Following the alphabet reform (1928–29), during which millions of Turks learned to read and write using Latin scripts, several pieces of legislation were enacted with the goal of securing women's rights. On April 3, 1930, women were granted the right to elect and be elected in municipal elections.

The same year, following the revolt that led to a massacre and the beheading of a young republican officer in Menemen by those demanding the return of the Sharia, all twenty-nine religious middle schools training students to become imams were closed, and the following year, the Directorate of Religious Affairs decided that the call to prayer should be said in Turkish. In 1934, women were granted the right to vote and stand as candidates in nationwide general elections.

Finally, in what some view as the final but crowning achievement of this glorious period, the Parliament gave its approval for the establishment of "Village Institutes" where, under a co-educational curriculum, students were trained and educated in various skills pertinent to rural life. This was to insure that many young graduates of these institutes would choose to stay near their homes.

◆   ◆   ◆

Following the death of Kemal Atatürk and the end of World War II, the trend to reverse the earlier achievements of the revolution began in earnest. The footsteps of the counter-revolution could be heard clearly following the general elections of 1946, during which the opposition "Demokrat" Party exploited the religious sensitivities of the public, and especially of the rural population. Gripped with a sense of panic, the party that always laid claim to the mantle of Atatürk began to dismantle, in quick succession, the various segments of the edifice that he had painstakingly built.

It began in the area of education, with the introduction of religious courses, the reopening of the *imam-hatip* schools, and the inauguration of faculties of theology in the universities. The village institutes, which had become a lightning rod for all fanatical religious movements, once again became ballast the regime thought it could toss out to regain altitude. First, they barred co-education, and then they collected from the school libraries all translated copies of world classics and burned them. Then, in 1948, the fear of losing the approaching general elections made them even more desperate, so they decided to close these remarkable, visionary, and, in many respects, uniquely revolutionary institutions. In 1950, hoping to stem the tide of religious support for the opposition, Atatürk's party reopened all religious convents (*tekke*) and the homes of religious recluses (*zaviye*).

Thus, the period leading to the 1950 general elections was marked by the resurgence of all sorts of reactionary forces. All political parties that formed during this period appealed to the public's religious sensitivities. The Party for National Development championed the establishment of an Islamic Union. The Party for Social Justice advocated a Union of World Muslims. The Party of Purity and Defense had no compunction declaring itself a religious political party. Another party, called The Party of Islamic Defense had set a goal of elevating Islam to a higher level. The Turkish Conservative Party proudly declared that its program was based on Islamic principles. Even the Party of Land, Property, and Free Enterprise pledged to support religion.

In hindsight, it is all too clear that the Kemalist movement had failed to educate and inform the public about the nature and role of secularism. The system was not yet fully accepted by the public and thus vulnerable to the opportunistic tactics of those who abused a Western-style democratic pluralistic model. By promising to bring religion back into the daily lives of the citizens these opportunists were appealing to the electorate's lowest common denominator.

The multi-party system became a race to the bottom, and parties competed to prove that they could deliver the most religious programs to the voters. And events followed each other quickly.

The counter-revolutionaries were gaining momentum, and their actions becoming more daring. Parliamentarians representing an Islamist party, the Party of National Liberation (Milli Selamet Partisi-MSP), dared to challenge established protocol and boycotted the ceremonies commemorating Atatürk's death. Sit-ins during the singing of the national anthem and the furling of the green flag of Islam became symbols of anti-republicanism. The race to the bottom reached a new depth when the republic ordered the lowering of the national flag on the occasion of the death of Ayatollah Khomeni of Iran.

◆   ◆   ◆

Appeasement never succeeds in the face of an implacable enemy who senses ultimate victory within its reach, and Turkey was no exception. The fanatics were on the march and one intellectual after another paid the ultimate price. Between

January and October 1990, Professors Muammer Aksoy, Çetin Emeç, and Turan Dursun, as well as Associate Professor Bahriye Üçok, were murdered by radical Islamists. Three years later, on January 24, 1993, one of the most outspoken defenders of the Republican/Kemalist cause, writer Uğur Mumcu, perished when a bomb planted under his car exploded.

However, the Kemalists were not the only target of the Islamist forces. Among others, the adherents of the "Alevi" sect of Islam were also the target of bloody attacks. In one that was particularly savage, on July 2, 1993, the fanatics attacked a group of Alevis congregating in a hotel in Sıvas to commemorate one of their illustrious scholars. Thirty-seven writers, artists, and politicians perished in an inferno caused by a group of arsonists. That particular weekend, the state security apparatus appeared to have gone fishing...

Meanwhile, insulting the memory and even the mother of Atatürk became a political sport. Politicians would unashamedly declare, without subtlety, that they were not born in Salonika (Atatürk's birthplace), nor were they a "son-of-a-whore!"

In 1994, a new actor took center stage. Having been elected mayor of Istanbul on the Islamist ticket of then Prime Minister Erbakan, Recep Tayyip Erdoğan opened the first meeting of the municipal council by reading the opening chapter of the Koran (Fatiha). The following year, the Municipal Council of Ankara, with an AKP majority, voted to replace the Hittite Sun, which was until then the logo of the city, with the profile of a mosque.

The killing of liberals and intellectuals continued unabated. On July 25, 1995, the head of the Gümüşhane Bar Association, Ali Günay, was gunned down by a radical Islamist. On October 21, 1999, another brilliant intellectual, Professor Ahmet Taner Kışlalı died from his wounds, and a year later the security chief of Diyarbakır, Gaffar Okkan, was ambushed and killed.

Following a lull of a few years the assassinations of those perceived to present a major obstacle to the implementation of the Islamist agenda raised its ugly head, once again, on December 2002. Historian, writer, academician Dr. Necip Hablemitoğlu was gun down in Ankara. He was actively assisting those fighting the activities of Fethullah Gülen and villagers opposed to gold mining activities pursued by the German Foundations. Three years later, in the spring of 2006, it was a broad daylight assault against the senior judges of the country's highest administrative court (Danıştay).

On May 17, 2006 an attacker with a murky past and suspicious motives entered a court building chanting "Allahu Akbar" (God is greatest) and sprayed bullets in a conference room, wounding four and killing one of the six judges present. The assailant was protesting a judicial decision on the wearing of the Muslim headscarf.

During the campaign for the November 2002 general elections and afterwards, in speeches and in interviews with the media, Erdoğan insisted that he and his followers had changed. What they had said in the past was no longer their policy goals. He said:" We have removed the shirt we were wearing before." The inevitable question arose: Is he a man of conviction or an opportunist? Or was he afraid of how the republican forces might react if things got out of control? What was the motivation for removing "that" shirt?

When asked if Turkey could become an Algeria, where the army waged a tenyear-long war against the Islamist insurgency, Erdoğan responded by describing their approach to Islamization: "Slowly, slowly…We are allowing things to be digested…"

These statements were incompatible with Article 81 of the constitution, which deals with the oath taken by all those elected to Parliament: "On my honor, I pledge before the great Turkish nation that I will defend the constitutional sovereignty of the nation; that I will remain committed to the rule of law, to the democratic and secular republic, and to Atatürk's principles and reforms; that I will remain faithful to the Constitution and I will not deviate from the goal of securing human rights and fundamental liberties for everyone."

The oath notwithstanding, AKP kept pushing the envelope. The Ministry of Foreign Affairs, in a directive issued to all embassies and consulates, demanded that they extend all possible help to the Schools of Fethullah Gülen (leader of the religious order Fethullahcı) and to the activities of Erbakan's National Vision (Milli Görüş) movement. In a recent briefing at the National Security Council meeting, the government was warned of a developing storm: "Twelve hundred foundations are involved in fundamentalist and reactionary activities. Some of these appear to involve universities. With financial resources of about $45 billion at their disposal, with about 500 private schools and 2000 dormitories, 500 classrooms, 35 holding companies, 245 radio and TV channels, and an estimated 13 thousands civil servants committed to the cause of an Islamist regime, the threat is very real."

However, the warning went unheeded. A far more direct admonishment was issued by the head of the Supreme Court of Appeal, Eraslan Özkaya who warned the public that demands for unlimited freedom of religion and conscience would prevent the state from being an arbiter on the issue of the separation of affairs of state and religion. He added that under such conditions anarchy would result followed by the establishment of a theocratic state with Sharia rules. The comments

drew the ire of the Prime Minister, who called them "unseemly and inappropri-
ate."

As the summer of 2005 began to yield to a fall that promised to be rather hot,
the only Kemalist forces so far resisting the onslaught were the president of the
republic, Ahmet Necdet Sezer, and the armed forces. The military was reminding
everyone that, according to the manual defining their duties and responsibilities,
they had the duty to defend and protect the republic and its reforms against both
external and internal enemies.

◆   ◆   ◆

A look at the present social landscape of Turkey reveals that the Kemalist
project is nowhere near complete. The republic, in its early years, had failed to
uproot and eliminate the feudal system in the east. The result was an "oligarchy"
where the feudal lords became the "representatives" of their subjects.

It is no surprise, then, that under such circumstances "land reform" meant
very little. Nor was it possible to fully integrate the female population into the
workforce and give them equal status with men. Celebrated historian scholar
Andrew Mango, describes the present-day dilemma faced by Turkey:

> Democracy, secularity, impersonal government, and management balanced by
> an active civil society developed gradually in the West where they had their
> origins. In contrast, Turkey is on a forced march to modernity, a march
> inspired by Atatürk, and sustained after his death, not by other reformers of
> his stature, but rather by the forces of globalization. (Andrew Mango, *The
> Turks Today*, 2005)

These forces of globalization were nowhere in sight when Turkey was developing a state-supported economy. Capital formation came, out of necessity,
through the creation of state enterprises and the awarding of contracts to the
friends of the regime. Many of today's major players, including some *Fortune* 500
heavyweights, made their early fortunes thanks to the largesse of the regime. Of
course, during World War II, being a sole source provider for almost anything
and everything helped too. It was not necessary to be a war profiteer to amass a
large fortune, but many did just that.

But today, under the forces of globalization ("free market capitalism"), sleazy
and corrupt practices, at all levels of society, have become more creative, more
difficult to control, and more corrosive. When one sees the wealth generated by
millions of honest and hardworking citizens being transferred abroad gradu-

ally—steadily but with great ease and stealth—one draws the inescapable conclusion: during the past quarter-century, with the help of globalization, corruption has visibly metastasized within the Turkish business community.

◆   ◆   ◆

The genesis of the Kemalist revolution is rooted in the pre-World War I period of the Ottoman Empire. At the turn of the century, Turkish railways, mines, and banks were increasingly coming under the control of European businesses. Ottoman sultans relied heavily on excessive borrowing of foreign capital. Sleazy and corrupt business ethics led to financial decadence accompanied by moral pollution and decay. As one might expect, this corrupt and ineffective regime inevitably failed to protect its own people. In the words of Winston Churchill, it was "rotted with misgovernment" and functioned as "a puppet government of Turkey." (Winston Churchill, *The World Crisis: The Aftermath*, 1929)

Today, one observes forboding similarities to the trends of yesteryears. Therefore, "finishing" the unfinished revolution of Kemal Atatürk is imperative for all those whose aim is genuine independence from the global forces working to assume control of the nation's economic and financial levers. Unfortunately, these forces have the willing submission and collaboration of entrenched and powerful local lobbies.

Since its inception as a republic, Turkey has accepted secularism as a guiding pillar in its march to modernity. To secure its acceptance by the public at large, the regime chose the classroom as the battleground where it would win the hearts and minds of future generations. Now one sadly observes that the goal of educating the young—a generation full of idealism and appreciative of the new society within which they were to take their place—was a partial failure.

Others have focused particularly on the role of secularism on the state's effort to control religious expression with the hope of depoliticizing religion and integrating it into the social life of the nation. Bekim Agai claimed that during the period of re-Islamisation, the role of the Directorate of Religious Affairs grew in a way not totally anticipated by the political and military circles. The creation of a Sunni "state religion" which, in turn, formed the basis for religious education in schools was one of the unintended consequences of such a policy. (Bekim Agai, *Islam and Kemalism in Turkey, www.Qantara.de*, May 15, 2005) Other experts have drawn similar conclusions by observing that the state had now established unchallenged monopoly over the definition of religion. A more serious consequence of such a state of affair has been the denial of representation within the system to the Alevites who constitute roughly 25–30 percent of the population.

According to Konny Dymond ("The Cult of Atatürk," *Christian Science Monitor*, 13 December, 2004), Izzettin Doğan, one of the Alevi Muslim community leaders in Turkey, said of Atatürk, "For the Alevi he is another kind of Imam Ali (the central figure of Shia Islam). In every Alevi home you will see a portrait of Atatürk." This assessment of the role of Alevis in today's Turkish society is seconded by Andrew Mango, who in his most recent book, *The Turks Today* wrote that they represent a "distinctively Turkish humanist Islam open to modernity." Söner Çagaptay, in her review of Andrew Mango's book, describes the Alevis as "liberal Muslims who profess a syncretic version of Islam laden with elements of Sufism and Shamanism, the Turks' pre-Islamic faith." She describes them as a group who shuns fundamentalism and cherishes secularism. (Söner Çagaptay, "March to Modernity," *Washington Post*, March 13, 2005)

Recently, the Alevis have been outspoken in their demand that their house of worship (*cemevi*) be recognized as separate and different than a mosque. Kazım Genç, president of Pir Sultan Abdal Cultural Associations and a member of the board of directors of the Alevi and Bektaşi Federation, asserted that the Alevis are not content to be a sect of Islam. (Interview with Neşe Düzel, *Radikal*, 10 October 2005) He stresses that their faith has dimensions that cover areas beyond religion, that it is a philosophy and a lifestyle. Regarding women, especially, he emphasizes the divide with Islam. He accused the Prime Minister of ignoring them and refusing to talk to them.

Moreover, according to Genç, as Mayor of Istanbul, Recep Tayyip Erdoğan has tried to demolish the Alevi *cemevi* located in Karacaahmet. Genç believes that the Prime Minister's religious formation and belief system are inimical towards the Alevis. The Wahabi-Sunni approach to the Alevi faith has been conditioned by such preconceived notions as "thou shall not eat what is butchered by an Alevi," "Alevis do not take baths; they are dirty," "Alevis are half-animal, half-human," "they spit into what they eat," and "he who kills an Alevi goes straight to heaven."

These statements were collected by the Pir Sultan Abdal Cultural Association in a survey conducted among one thousand Alevis across the Anatolian countryside. The stereotypical definition of what an Alevi is or isn't, inevitably, has developed into full-scale discrimination. Today, there are no Alevi among the eighty-one provincial governors. Of the four hundred general directors appointed by the state, none are Alevi. Finally, the prime minister's ruling party, AKP, is represented in Parliament by 356 deputies, none are Alevi. The Office of Religious

Affairs is the third most populous ministry. It has one hundred thousand person-nel, but no Alevi. Undeniably, frustration is building up among the 20–25 mil-lion Alevis. Even after they acquire the land upon which to build a *cemevi*, city ordinances are used to deny them the requisite permit on the ground that for "Muslims," the house of worship is the "mosque"' and therefore construction permits for such a building are not allowed. It is generally accepted that about one in every three Turks is of the Alevi faith. Yet, today there is a grand total of about one hundred *cemevi*s compared to 87000 mosques—the equivalent of one thousandth of one percent!

The image of the Prime Minister, both in and out of the country, suffers from a certain lack of clarity. It is caused partly by the amount of unwelcomed baggage he has brought to the office from his earlier years as a fiery and opportunist Islamist politician. Especially embarrassing, was his dealings with some of the most ques-tionable characters whose names have been linked to Islamist terror networks. Pos-ing to photographers while kneeling at the feet of Gulbuddin Hikmatyar, the Taliban ally who is now roaming the hills of Afganistan pursued by Nato forces, is not something Recep T. Erdoğan would like us to remember. Steven Stalinsky, the executive director of the Middle East Media Research Institute, reminds the reader of the significance of such a posture: "It is important to recognize that the signifi-cance of sitting at one's feet, in Islamic tradition, implies spiritual submission." (Turkey: A New Al-Qaeda State?, *Front Page,* March 25, 2005)

Towards the end of 2005, the Prime Minister, who until then had refrained from discussing this very question, attempted to explain his position. But the explanations proved to be baseless. Indeed, Hikmatyar was not visiting Turkey on an official capacity, as the prime minister claimed, but rather as the guest of the Islamist Refah Party, of which Erdoğan was the leader for the Province of Istanbul. The man at the knee of whom he was sitting then is now the hard-line Islamist leader of Hizb-u Islami Gulbuddin and one of the key targets of the U.S. forces operating in the Kunar region of Eastern Afghanistan, adjacent to the tribal areas of neighboring Pakistan. Gulbuddin Hikmatyar is believed to be working closely with a Taliban commander known as Ahmad Shah and an Arab called Abu Ikhlas al-Misri, said to be the al-Qaeda's leader in the region.

More recently another shady character's name has been linked to the Prime Minister. The man, Yasin El Kadi, who was formally accused by the United Nations of financing terrorist organizations and whose assets have been frozen in various countries, including the United States, was described by the Prime Minister as a benevolent philantropist. Testifying as a character witness, he declared: "I believe in him as much as I would believe in myself."

◆   ◆   ◆

AKP represents a movement that inherited an anti-secular pro-Sharia tradition, its founders and leadership cadres being the product of a party (Refah) ordered closed by the Constitutional Court for activities incompatible with the secularism clause of the constitution. The present membership of the party are mostly linked to one of the three major Sunni religious orders: Nakşibendi, Fethullahcı, or Süleymancı.

Prof. Şerif Mardin, chairman of Islamic Studies at the American University, in an interview with the Turkish daily *Milliyet* (28 February 2005), intimated that, for all practical purposes, Turkey's present regime is composed of elements of the Nakşibendi religious order, an offshoot of the Nurcu movement.

In fact, the Nakşibendi brotherhood and its leader, Said-i-Nursi, became the symbol of religious opposition against the secular Turkish nation-state. His criticism focused on the state's implementation of secularism and nationalism. Paradoxically, the republic not only tolerated but welcomed members of the Nakşibendi Order. They held important positions in Parliament and in the state bureaucracy (Camilla Trud Nereid, "In the Light of Said Nursi-Turkish Nationalism and the Religious Alternative", *Bergen Studies on the Middle East and Africa V.4*).

These days, the Prime Minister takes great pains to denounce his early ideology. The party describes itself as a middle-class conservative movement, much like the German Christian Democratic Union. They profess to be business friendly, calling for the privatization of most of the national enterprises.

Turkey's relationships with the United States and the European Union, of which it aspires to become a member, are central to Turkey's international role. Addressing a conference at the War Academies in Istanbul on April 14, 2004, President Ahmet Necdet Sezer stressed the importance of the country's Kemalist ideology and the principle of secularism as a fundamental element of the Turkish society. (*APS Diplomat Recorder*, 17 April 2004, v.60, Issue: 16) He strongly stressed that "any attempts to describe secular Turkey as an Islamic Republic or to have people subconsciously adopt some models with meaningless qualifications like 'moderate Islam' are unacceptable." He went on to add, that "since moderate Islam is not the regime of the Republic of Turkey, it is understood that some circles envisaged a new regime for our state." The president admits that such a "moderate" Islamist regime can be considered a progress for other Muslim countries, but reminds the audience that "it is nothing but a fundamentalist model for Turkey."

A staunch Kemalist, the president's words appeared to be directed to some strategic allies. Especially when he reminded his audience of the contradiction between the concept of a moderate Islamic society and the democratization of such a society: "Any attempt to bring together a theocratic state and democracy is contradicted by history and science." He further argued that the "principle of secularism is one of the basic values forming the Republic of Turkey" and "those who propose a moderate Islam model for Turkey are ignoring the irrevocable principle of the secular state enshrined within the constitution."

In a newsletter dated May 12, 2003, *APS Diplomat Strategic Balance in the Middle East* (v.5.issue:4) described Turkey's predicament:

> A locomotive with two engines pulling in opposite directions: the military engine pushing in the secular direction, while the engine of the ruling AKP is beginning to pull towards the Islamist path. Unless one side reduces power, the locomotive will remain motionless and if both sides increase power, then the locomotive may be split in two.

◆   ◆   ◆

The dichotomy between upholding the Kemalist principle of secularism and being mindful not to alienate its Islamist wing has always been a challenge for AKP. Initially referred to as the "Homecoming Law," the last in a series of "repentance statutes" Turkey enacted over the years (with limited success), the so-called Amnesty Law, was designed to allow the PKK terrorists to demobilize and return to civilian life while avoiding prosecution. But during the debates in Parliament, the bill was hijacked and broadened so that Islamist terrorists would also qualify under it. Following the Istanbul bombings of a synagogue, the HSBC bank, and the British consulate, the police arrested a number of suspects, who were later charged. Several of those arrested were members of the Turkish Hizbullah and IBDA-C Islamic terrorist movements and they had filed applications to qualify under the Amnesty Law.

Another example of the party's split personality was on display during the days leading to the fateful December 17, 2004, EU summit. There the leaders of the EU were to eventually issue an invitation to Turkey to begin discussions concerning Turkey's accession to the Union. But back home, in a parliament were quite a few deputies have, in addition to their lawfully wedded wives, a second "wife" (*kuma*) sanctioned by Sharia laws, AKP attempted to criminalize adultery. The furious reaction from the EU Commission and in particular from Günter Verheugen, the man responsible for preparing the report to the summit, forced the Islamists to retract. But the damage had already been done. The inevitable question in many minds was whether AKP was sincere when declaring its intent to become part of Europe.

The final episode occurred more recently. During parliamentary debates on the final text of the new Turkish Penal Code (May 26, 2005) members amended Article 263. Penalties against those found guilty of teaching the Koran in unlicensed (i.e., illegal) schools were reduced to nominal fines. These schools had already caught the attention of the authorities in 1997, and in the year 2000 they were put under the supervision of the Ministry of National Education. Now, especially during the summer months under the guise of "summer training schools," they will claim to offer courses on a wide variety of subjects, from carpet weaving and sewing to accounting and computer skills, when in reality their goal is to help students memorize the Koran, in Arabic.

AKP cadres belong to a fundamentalist school of Islam and are not in tune with modern developments in the field of Islamic theology. In fact, Reza Aslan, the Iranian-American scholar of comparative religion, argues that a sweeping Islamic reformation is already underway in the Muslim world. Especially reformist is his argument that "the notion that historical context should play no role in the interpretation of the Koran—that what applied to Mohammad's community applies to all Muslim communities for all time—is simply an untenable position in every sense." (Reza Aslan, *No God but God,* 2005)

But with each passing day, undeterred, the Islamists are flexing their muscles, and the locomotive with two engines is sputtering.

2

A BATTLE FOR
THE HEARTS AND MINDS

Of all the reforms Atatürk was engaged in, perhaps the most challenging was that of gender equality. Given the status of women in most Muslim countries, the task must have been monumental. As Lord Kinross describes it, the Kemalist revolution treaded the issue very circumspectly: "It was one thing in Turkey to clap a hat on the head of a man. It was quite another to tear the veil off a woman. No Law for the Maintenance of Order, no Independence Tribunals would enforce such a metamorphosis." (Lord Kinross, *Atatürk-The Rebirth of a Nation, 1964*)

Unfortunately, here, too, we find an "unfinished" reform. Many foreigners, while visiting Istanbul spend some time shopping in the "Covered Bazaar" near Beyazıt, at the heart of the historic district. The tourist buses will drop them at the entrance to the Nuruosmaniye Mosque. The street (by the same name) is lined with some of the most expensive carpet and antique dealers in town. The pedestrians walking the broad sidewalks are not unlike any you would encounter in the more modern districts of town.

However, if you take a slightly different route and decide to enter the bazaar through its northern gates by walking, or rather climbing, along the hilly street called Mahmutpaşa Yokuşu, the picture you see would be quite different. The difference is even more striking if you venture to some of the less visited corners of the old town, like Fatih, Topkapı, or Eyüp.

In each of these districts, women are mostly covered, some from head to toe, in their black dresses, while others even have their faces shuttered behind a veil. Considering that Istanbul women are supposed to be the most emancipated in the nation, one must conclude that the emancipation of women is an unfinished project and that it would be quite unrealistic to expect the Islamists to do anything about it.

Inevitably, the same question comes to mind: what went wrong? The answer lies in the republic's failure to offer equal educational opportunities to girls, coupled with its inability to eradicate the feudal structure in the east and meaningfully engage in the economic development of the eastern half of the country. When economic opportunities failed to materialize in their provinces, many families moved to the big urban centers of the west, surrounding the cities with ever-growing slums and bringing with them their conservative customs, religiosity, and social values and attitudes.

One of the more disturbing trends that followed was the society's tolerance of violence against women. The pattern is almost identical to the one German social scientists have reported after studying the so-called *gastarbeiter* or "guest workers" imported from Eastern Turkey right after WWII and who chose to stay in Germany. In many respects, when compared with their countrymen living in Turkey, they were found to be even more conservative and far less adaptable to the lifestyle of their adopted land.

To illustrate the point:

1.   Between October 2004 and March 2005, five Turkish women were murdered in Berlin. Police evidence indicates that all five murders were "honor killings." The total is close to 55 for the period of the past six years. Family members, reacting to a woman's refusal to enter an arranged marriage or to her decision to liberate herself from the traditional subservient role expected of her, decide to execute her in order to "cleanse the honor" of the family. The shooting is carried out by a male member of the family, preferably a minor, who would then benefit from the leniency of the court.

2.   In Adana, a brother forced his fourteen-year-old sister to submit, at a state clinic, to a virginity test, which proves negative. During the ensuing argument, he proceeded to stab her repeatedly (*Radikal,* March 8, 2005).

3.   On Sunday March 6, 2005 in Istanbul, during demonstrations related to International Women's Day, police kicked and beat with truncheons women lying on the ground, all before the unforgiving eyes of television cameras. The brutality of the attacks shocked the members of the visiting Troika of EU foreign ministers from Luxembourg, Belgium, and Britain. The initial reaction of the Turkish government was that there was grave provocation and that the police's reaction was no more severe than what transpired in Genoa earlier during anti-globalization demon-

strations. Besides, said the PM, International Women's Day is on March 8, so what were these women doing on Sunday, March 6? (*Cumhuriyet*, March 9, 2005)

4. In an interview with battered women staying in a "shelter", or "safe house," near Istanbul, the daily *Vatan* (March 8, 2005) detailed the heart-wrenching saga of a wife who, after taking a beating for ten years, decided to leave, aware of the potentially life-threatening consequences of her decision. Another woman who was forced to marry at the age of fourteen is now being commanded to return to her husband under the threat of violence. Not only is she refusing to obey, but she is defiantly attending courses to learn to read and write, determined as she is to work so she can earn her own living and support her children.

5. A young girl was forced to marry her pedophile rapist at the age of thirteen, and when she refused the demand of her father-in-law (who also raped her) to enter prostitution, he had her nose cut off. (Suna Erdem reports from Istanbul to the *Times of London*, June 2, 2005)

◆   ◆   ◆

Not a day passes by without the story of a gruesome attack perpetrated against a wife, a daughter, or a girlfriend. When it comes to gender-biased violence, Turkey's report card is filled with failing notes.

A survey carried out under the supervision of Dr. Aytekin Sır, professor of psychiatry in the School of Medicine at the University of Dicle, in Southeastern Turkey (*Hürriyet*, October 18, 2005), reveals the enormity of the cultural and social gap between the east and the west of the country. According to Professor Aytekin Sır, 37.4 percent of the respondents declared, unequivocally, their support for the practice of "honor killing" in cases where women have committed adultery. Another 21.6 percent favored "alternative" punishments, such as the severing of an ear or the nose, or forced suicide. To the question "Who should carry out the punishment?" 64 percent said that it was the duty of the husband. In presenting his results, Professor Sır emphasized that he has been working on this subject in the region of S.E. Anatolia for fifteen years and that prior to administering the survey, he and his ten men team identified the groups they would target, focusing their work on villages inhabited by Kurds, Zazas, Arabs, and Alevis.

The extensive comments on the Internet concerning this report turned out to be quite revealing. Many southeastern readers questioned the accuracy of the findings. Some claimed that probably close to 90 percent of the citizenry in the southeast would favor honor killing. Others blamed the close proximity of Arab-Sunni culture. Someone warned Europe, in tongue-in-cheek fashion, of the impending arrival of ear-shaving, nose-cutting hordes to make the European multi-cultural society a reality.

In an article by Thierry Oberle titled "Little Family Killings in the South-East Anatolia" ("Petits meurtres en famille dans le Sud-Est anatolien," *Le Figaro*, 3 October 2005), Professor Aytekin Sır is quoted as stating that in the Province of Diyarbakır, the rate of suicide for women is double that for men. According to Professor Sır, the highest number of suicides among women occur between the ages of fifteen and twenty-five, the age group when girls are most often forced into marriage. The most common forms of suicide are by shooting, poisoning, agricultural pesticides, or rat poison. In cases where suicide is forced upon these young women, those responsible are rarely apprehended. An attorney from Diyarbakır, Zülal Erdoğan confirms that it is difficult to prove that a girl has been forced to commit suicide when the whole family is silent or, as it happens sometime, a twelve-year-old tells the court that he accidentally killed his mother.

In the same article, *Le Figaro* tells the tragic story of two lovers, Şemsiye Allak and Halil Açıl, who were stoned to death following the pregnancy of Şemsiye. A few months after the death of the couple, the two Kurdish families were reconciled during a banquet (!) organized by the elders of the tribe and the leaders (!) of the City of Mardin.

The story of three women, each from a different corner of the land, is just as revealing. All three had appealed to the courts for protection against their violent husbands, and the courts had obliged. But all three suffered a similar fate: one was stabbed to death, another was gunned down, and the third was burned to death—all at the hands of their husbands.

◆   ◆   ◆

It's impossible to improve women's political station without improving the education, economic participation, and economic opportunities of women within Turkish society. The paucity of female representation in Parliament is just one of many indictments on the present political elite.

Given the scope and parameters of the problem confronting the nation it is all the more disconcerting to watch the present regime direct all its energy at ensuring women wear the headscarf in public places. Nothing could better illustrate the irony of this obsession than the photographs published in the Turkish media concerning a World Economic Forum in Jordan dealing with women's issues. Emine Erdoğan, wife of Prime Minister Erdoğan, was shown along the wives of other Muslim world leaders: Benazir Butto, former PM of Pakistan; Suzan Mubarek, wife of the president of Egypt; Esma Esad, wife of the president of Syria; Dr. Siti Hasmah Mohamed Ali, wife of former PM of Malaysia; and Randa Berri, wife of the Lebanese parliamentary spokesman. Only Mrs. Erdoğan had her hair covered under a scarf, which closed her ears and most of her neck in a style called *sıkma-baş*(squeezed head). In the hot weather of Jordan, she was wearing a full-length coat, all the way to her ankles. No other guests had their hair covered, and many were wearing pants.

In an even greater irony, in her presentation about female empowerment, she praised almost all of the social reforms carried out during the Kemalist revolution without ever mentioning the name of Kemal Atatürk or that of the secular Republic. Yet she found an opportunity to invite the audience to draw inspiration from the achievements of a businesswoman named Hatice, whose husband went on to receive the word of God and become the Prophet Mohammed!

Coinciding with the Jordan conference, the World Economic Forum issued a comprehensive report (*Women's Empowerment: Measuring the Global Gender Gap*, May 2005). Many Turkish writers and intellectuals were shocked to learn that Turkey was ranked fifty-seventh among fifty-eight countries with respect to the gender gap. This should not have been surprising, as five years earlier, the Turkish Association of Industrialists and Businessmen (TÜSIAD) had issued an equally critical report. In it, they pointed out that the percentage of women in the labor force had shrunk from 72 percent in 1955 to 29 percent in 1999, with the bulk (75 percent) of women still working in the agricultural sector.

The overall picture is bleak. Nationally, six out of every seven illiterates are women, and it is apparent that Turkey has a long way to go before achieving a genuine equality of opportunity among the sexes. The solution can not be found in the Koran, and the Islamist approach to women issues is enough to cause one to despair about the future.

Turkey's national averages in the areas of human development are extremely skewed. Human poverty and gender bias are hidden among the overall statistics covering the whole of the country. There are enormous disparities when comparing the eastern and western part of the land. In the eastern part of the country, long-term unemployment, a shorter life span, an income below the national poverty line, and a high rate of illiteracy are evidence of serious human poverty.

These trends reinforce economic stagnation, low human development and a general unwillingness to improve women's lot in all areas of human endeavor.

It has been twenty years since Turkey became a signatory to the Convention on the Elimination of All Kinds of Discrimination against Women (CEDAW). Since 1990, the General Directorate on the Status and Problems of Women has had a specific mandate to insure the rightful status of women and gender equality in social, economic, cultural, and political fields. In addition, a United Nations funded program called the Shelter Homes for Women Violence Victims addressed such primary issues as women's rights, empowerment of women, women's unequal access to resources and productive employment, institutional impediments, and women's lack of access to decision-making and effective participation in political, social, cultural, and economic processes.

But the issue of the headscarf still remains a hot topic. Today's Islamists maintain that Islam has adapted to modernity and, therefore, for women to be allowed to go to school wearing a headscarf is nothing more than an individual's basic human right. Interestingly, the headscarf controversy goes a long way back. Almost fifteen years ago, the religious daily *Zaman*, the mouthpiece of the followers of Fethullah Gülen, the leader of the religious order of the same name and who is presently living in the United States, declared on its front page, "You cannot uncover my head as long as it is not severed from this body!" In those days, daily demonstrations in the form of sit-ins were quite common. But something interesting happened as soon as AKP assumed the responsibility of government. All demonstrations were abruptly stopped and the government chose to take a wait-and-see approach.

The problem was that there were legal obstacles against their plans to push for a change by fiat. Indeed, the Superior Court for Administration (Danıştay) declared the use of the headscarf in schools to be in violation of the principle of unity in education, as stated in the National Education Act. The Constitutional Court, for its part, found the use of the headscarf in schools to be in violation of the principle of secularism enshrined in the constitution.

Recent surveys indicate that almost all men who expect their wives to wear the headscarf belong to one of several religious orders and brotherhoods. That alone seems to support the argument that the headscarf is the symbol of membership in a religious order rather than the symbol of one's individual right to religion. For an illustration of the intellectual frame of mind of those leading present-day Turkey, one needs to peruse the contents of books authored by officials of the Office of Religious Affairs. It's not unusual to read statements such as "The veil is the honor of a woman, and any deviation from the practice of being veiled could lead to immoral relations…"

◆   ◆   ◆

But it would be unfair to point the finger solely to the AKP regime as the initiators of the anti-Kemalist counterrevolution. The gradual erosion of Kemalist reforms had its beginning in the period from 1950 to 1960. Prime Minister Adnan Menderes is today remembered as the leader who appealed to his followers' ego by saying, "Should you desire, you can bring back the Caliphate!" But more damaging has been his decision to allow the call to prayer to be made in Arabic and his introduction of compulsory religious teaching of Islam. He was the godfather of the shift towards political Islam, but he was not even a practicing Muslim.

Süleyman Demirel was the first prime minister who would pray in his office. Demirel, who was disparagingly called Morrison Süleyman by some of his detractors (an allusion to his relation with the American consulting engineering firm Morrison Knudsen), has openly expressed the belief that except for verses pertaining to worldly and individual relationships—about 230—most of the remaining verses of the Koran are still valid and could be the basis of the law of the land. According to Demirel, the inapplicability of those verses and the fact that they had been replaced by modern jurisprudence should not diminish the fact that we are still governed by Islamic Law.

Throughout the years, Demirel has been supported by the followers of Said-i Kürdi (a.k.a., Said-i Nursi, since he was born in the village of Nurs) as well as by the adherents of the Fethullahcı and Nakşibendi brotherhoods. Demirel regularly boasted that he was the prime minister under whose watch the greatest number of religious schools (*imam-hatip*) had opened.

If we are going to rank prime ministers by their contributions to the counterrevolution aimed at undermining the Kemalist reforms, Necmettin Erbakan deserves first place.

Erbakan founded Milli Nizam (National Order) in the 1970s. When the authorities closed it for anti-constitutional activities, he founded Refah (Welfare). The party openly declared political warfare against what it called "the dictatorship of the secular republic." In 1994, addressing the party's parliamentary group, he was in a fighting mood: "There is no doubt about the final outcome: Refah will come to power and with it a just order. The only question is whether the transition period will be hard or soft, bloody or peaceful. Sixty million will decide which path."

Once again, the party was found to be engaged in activities aimed at bringing down the democratic order. The appeal to the European Court for Human Rights was rebuffed when the court declared that every state had the right to defend its institutions and that the calls to jihad by the leaders of Refah and their demand for a dual-track legal system—contemporary law and Sharia—were contrary to the European Treaty for Human Rights.

Another colorful character, the darling of the Nakşibendi and Süleymancı brotherhoods but also the favorite of the American military and business interests, was Turgut Özal. He was the first president of the republic who converted the blue room of the presidential palace into a prayer room (*mescid*), the first to make a pilgrimage to Mecca, the first to advocate the adoption of creationism in lieu of Darwinism as part of the high school curriculum. His tenure saw Turkey totally surrender to the International Monetary Fund and, by extension, to the dictates of foreign capital.

The speaker of the Parliament, Bülent Arınç, is another hard core Islamist. A dangerous demagogue, a virulent anti-secularist, he has consistently advocated a redefinition of 'secularism' that would be more to his liking. Not the way it is defined in the Constitution—the formal, legal separation of religion from politics-but rather the freedom to exercise the religious rituals of a given sect without interference from the State.

His ambition is to become the next head of the Republic. If and when that happens we will all know that the second Republic has finally arrived. The only comforting assurance you hear about such an outcome is: 'Have no fear! Turkey will never become another Iran. Initially she may look more like Malaysia and a few years later become another Pakistan.'

◆   ◆   ◆

This brings us to Recep Tayyip Erdoğan. As the leader of Refah for the province of Istanbul, he proudly posed kneeling before the Afghan Islamist Gulbuddin Hikmatyar, who is still at large in the mountains of Afghanistan. In later years, Erdoğan would declare, "We are engaged in a battle to impose a new order within this society." And he was never shy of bringing the idea of martyrdom: "Let your children die in defense of Allah's order rather than in the southeast fighting the PKK." Not to miss any opportunity to insult Kemal Atatürk: "They would go to visit his mausoleum without having any idea about his days of reckoning." Addressing the electorate: "You should consider the matter carefully. Even if on the way to the ballot box you may think that sovereignty belongs to the people, in fact and in spirit, sovereignty belongs unconditionally to Allah." And finally, in the matter of uncovered women: "Is it because of the Sharia which they have lambasted since 1924 that Turkey has turned into a whorehouse?"

A few years later, he was openly challenging the secular state: "They keep lamenting that secularism is on the way out. Well, as long as that is the wish of the nation, of course secularism will end!" He would also challenge the separation of mosque and state: "One cannot be secular and Muslim at the same time. You are either a Muslim or secular." Erdoğan did not hesitate to give to his elected position as the mayor of Istanbul a far broader interpretation: "I am the imam of Istanbul." And in the fateful speech in Siirt that eventually landed him in jail, he said, "Minarets are our bayonets/domes are our helmets/and the faithful our soldiers." When he declared, "Islam is our point of reference," there was no doubt in anyone's mind what he felt should *not* be the point of reference: "In the future of Turkey there can be no place for Kemalism or any other ideology." He went further by mounting a frontal attack against the very republic he wished to lead: "Let me say that the concept of a republic, for the people and by the people, has very little significance for us. I am of the opinion that in Turkey the principle of republic should yield its place to a participatory regime and the principle of secularism ought to fuse with Islam." He was consistent on this score: "The Ottomans managed to keep together all thirty different ethnic groups through the idea of a 'nation of Islam' (*ümmet*), and we will do the same through the union of faith!"

For a while it was reasonable to wait and see if indeed Recep Tayyip Erdoğan had changed from the days when he was the "fire and brimstone" preacher of the religious right. He did say, before audiences, that he and his followers had shed their old shirts and were the new face of the Islamist movement in Turkey. After watching and giving him the slack he had asked for, it is now apparent that we are watching a classic power grab, albeit a gradual one, beginning with the placement of his cronies and trusted supporters in key positions of the state and followed by the "salami tactic" of eating away at the edifice of the secular Republic, one slice at a time.

For example, the names of many high-level bureaucrats submitted for approval to the president were turned down by President Sezer, who found them either unqualified or unsuitable for the offices for which they were proposed. The government's response was quite illustrative of their contempt for the secular president and the state's present structure. Rather than withdraw the names of the candidates, they used a loophole in the system to make temporary appointments, designating the same bureaucrats as "acting director," "acting chairman," etc. Some of these appointees have served in their "temporary" capacity for well over two years, in complete disregard for both the letter and the spirit of the law.

Nevertheless, the issue appears to be driving a wedge between the president and the prime minister. In early June 2005, the office of the president disclosed the text of a letter dated March 7, 2005, addressed from the president to the prime minister. In it, the president refers to Article 128 of the constitution, charging civil service employees with proper conduct of public service, and to State Law 657, regulating the hiring and employment of such civil servants. Referring to an opinion of the Superior Court for Administration, he emphasizes the temporary nature of "acting" appointments. Furthermore, referring to another court opinion, he stresses that those employed in an "acting" capacity must meet the same minimum qualifications of education and competence as those serving permanent posts. He concluded by emphasizing the temporary nature of any government as opposed to the permanency of the State which civil servants represent, and by calling for respect for the rule of law.

The next day, talking to reporters, the Prime Minister said that those who take political risks should be free to do as they please. After all, it is the electorate who would finally decide their fate. Unfortunately, the answer was not an answer, for if respect for the rule of law means anything, everybody, including the politicians, should obey the law. The electorate is neither judge nor jury.

◆   ◆   ◆

There is another issue where AKP is determined to show its green colors: the development of an Islamic private sector in accord with the decisions taken at the 1999 annual meeting of the Islamic Development Bank. The Organization for the Development of an Islamic Private Sector has been in operation since July 2000. As a founding member of the organization, Turkey has been a signatory to the accord since September 2003. The Turkish Parliament was now being asked to ratify the treaty.

Under the treaty, the development of a private sector that will comply with the rules of Islam (i.e., Sharia) is to be encouraged. One may see this as odd considering that Turkey is a secular land. The principle of equality before the law cannot justify the coexistence of two private sectors, side by side, where one is encouraged and developed while the other is left free to operate as it wishes. Furthermore, the bank will have a Committee for Islamic Jurisprudence, whose job will be to determine if an area proposed for investment is in agreement with Islam. In other words, if an investment does not agree with the tenets of Islam, it won't be supported.

You might ask yourselves about the reaction of the Association of Turkish Industrialists and Businessmen (TÜSIAD). They have not said a word about the issue. Maybe they don't believe in the vaunted free market economy anymore and are careful not to upset their relations with the powers to be! A "free" market economy in the hands of "not so free" businessmen…

The true color of the party is a serious matter. The party claims to be a conservative centrist movement. However, to some observers it has all the attributes of a classical Islamist movement and that it is merely trying to project a European profile for the purpose of achieving entry into the EU.

All the evidence uncovered so far suggests that the Islamist character of the party is in ascendancy. It would be appropriate to remind ourselves that all the terrorists who carried out the bloody attacks of the past few years in the name of Turkish Hizbullah have been Turkish citizens, educated in state-supervised religious schools (*imam-hatip*).

One new marker has been reported in the media. In early June 2005, in the Istanbul daily *Hürriyet*, Emin Çölaşan, author, columnist, and one of the giants of Turkish media, reported on the content of a questionnaire used to survey the parents in all primary schools throughout the capital city of Ankara. The parents were asked to provide "true" or "false" answers to certain statements. Here are some examples:

- One must believe in the existence of Allah.

- There is life after death.

- Everything told in the Koran is true.

- Mohammed is the prophet of Allah.

- Praying five times a day is important for me.

- Religious edicts will not change with changing conditions.

- One should refrain from transactions involving interest payment.

- Polygamy agrees with the tenets of Islam.

- Angels will not visit a house where there are pictures.

- Civil marriage is null and void unless accompanied by a religious one.

- The faith of those who fail to pray five times a day is weak.

- One who fails to participate in the Friday prayer cannot be considered a Moslem.

- It is forbidden for men to wear gold.

- Wearing eau de cologne will make one unclean.

This true-false questionnaire was prepared by a doctoral student in the Religious Studies program at Ankara University. It was forwarded to all primary schools of the city. Following an outcry, the Ministry of National Education, which oversees such activities, disassociated itself from the part of the questionnaire addressed to the parents. But once again we witnessed the usual pattern of two steps backward followed by one step forward.

Ten years ago, the same reactionary forces attempted to amend the policy governing the rules of admission to the various military colleges by removing the clause barring religious school (*imam-hatip*) graduates from applying. Just a small fraction of each year's graduating class applies for admission to the theology faculties of the universities or to the institutes for Islamic studies. The rest seek admission into the College of Political Sciences or the School of Law.

Now why would the graduates of *imam-hatip* schools prefer to serve in the armed forces or as judges or provincial administrators after having prepared themselves for a career in the field of religious affairs? Today, only six percent of the civil servants employed in the Directorate of Religious Affairs have an earned degree from an institution of higher learning. Only a little more than half of all the personnel employed in the directorate is graduates of religious schools (*imam-hatip*). The day when this religiously-trained army of administrators takes over the administration of the provinces, the courts, and the police and state security apparatus, the Kemalist dream of a secular regime will end. It will mark the beginning of the "second Republic."

The blueprint for creating this second Republic by surreptitiously seizing all the key posts of the State has been advocated by several Muslim scholars who, over the years, have been subtle, shrewd, and patient in their advocacy of a soft takeover. Among the various offshoots of the Nakşibendi-Nurcu brotherhood, some are radical and transparent, and others are very secretive. But none can compare, in terms of shrewdness and sophistication, with the movement led by Fethullah Gülen. The movement is an integral part of the so-called Moderate Islam Project, which has been conceived and promoted actively by the neo-conservatives in the United States administration.

◆   ◆   ◆

Over the years, various Islamic groups have proposed different routes to achieve their ultimate goal of securing power in the name of Islam. For example, the German Islamists affiliated with Cemalettin Kaplan consider it heresy to attempt to form a party. Those who are followers of the Party of God (Hizb-ul-lah) consider terror a legitimate weapon in the struggle to gain power. Necmettin Erbakan and his successive parties (Milli Nizam, Refah, Saadet) have always maintained that the ultimate goal is to secure power by the ballot box, although he has also intimated that eventually the battle could be "bloody." Fethullah and his followers, on the other hand, have always advocated seizing the state by infiltrating its various organs, i.e., securing its key posts. The movement is active among the various Turkish university faculties. Furthermore, it has made major investments in secondary education both in Turkey as well as abroad—in the Turkic Republics, in the autonomous republics within Russia, in the Balkans, among the Turkish *diaspora* living in Europe, in Africa, and even in the United States. They control major media outlets, both print and electronic, and finally, they have the support of the only superpower in the world, the United States, where Fethullah Gülen has been living for the past eight years.

The movement, through one of its many foundations, the Turkish Journalists and Writers Foundation, sponsors an event called the "Abant Platform." Although a semiannual event, on certain occasions it holds conferences centered on a particular topic. Following one held in Brussels on the occasion of the EU Summit where Turkish candidacy was discussed and a date was finally announced regarding the adhesion talks (October 3, 2005), another conference was organized in Washington, D.C., on April 19, 2005, co-hosted by the John Hopkins Paul H. Nitze School of Advanced International Studies (SAIS) and Turkey's Journalists and Writers Foundation, on the topic "Islam, Secularism, and Democracy: The Turkish Experience." With Fethullah Gülen serving as honorary chairman, these gatherings are a showpiece for the political clout of the movement.

Mehmet Aydın, minister of state in charge of religious affairs and a dark horse candidate for the next presidency of the republic delivered the keynote address. Another minister of state, this one in charge of economic affairs, Ali Babacan, who more recently was appointed chief negotiator for the EU accession negotiations, provided the opening remarks during the second day. There was even an opposition parliamentarian, Kemal Derviş, who is credited by some with saving

Turkey from its worst economic crisis, in 2001, and who has since resigned his post to become the number-three man at the United Nations headquarters.

Several academics with strong ties to the Fethullah movement presented papers praising the Turkish model of a tolerant and democratic moderate Islam. The Foundation had a media representative, Cengiz Çandar, from the conservative daily *Tercüman* (now *Bugün*). He seems to be a regular fixture at these Abant platforms, having also participated at the previous one as a panel member. He is an unabashed advocate of United States policy and gained some notoriety by writing, the day Bagdad fell to the U.S. Army, "I wish I was in Bagdad today!"

That day, listening to the speakers, one would have been totally unaware that Fethullah Gülen, the honorary chairman of the conference, had been charged, on August 31, 2000, by the Republican prosecutor of the State Security Tribunal, with organizing an illegal religious order for the purpose of changing the secular structure of the state into a theocratic Islamic one. The prosecutor stated that the goal was to pack the civil service rolls with elements educated and trained in Fethullah Gülen's schools and classrooms—in particular, the judiciary, the civil administration, and the military.

To support his arguments, the prosecutor, Nuh Mete Yüksel, presented to the court the transcripts of several video cassettes, on which Fethullah Gülen instructs his followers to lay low until the most opportune time. He explicitly underlines the need to be patient: "Any premature action on your part would cause them to crush your head, just as it happened in Algeria...Any move must be considered premature until you have secured all power centers into your camp...You must make every effort to advance within the bureaucracy, in the judicial, administrative or any other state institution, without making your presence felt but moving with stealth within the arteries of such institutions." By then, Gülen, who claimed the tapes had been tampered with, had already left the country, ostensibly for medical reasons.

Gülen's religious group controls 88 foundations, 20 associations, 128 private schools, 218 companies, 129 classrooms (and about 500 dormitories), 17 publications (one of which is in English), 1 daily (with an average circulation of quarter of a million), 1 TV station, 2 national radio stations, a financial institution offering interest-free service, and an insurance company. The group is extremely active abroad, operating in thirty-five countries. They include six universities, 236 high schools, 2 elementary schools, 8 language and computer centers, 6 university entrance preparation centers, and 21 student dormitories.

Some recent developments have cast serious clouds over these institutions. According to the daily *Cumhuriyet* (February 9, 2006), nearly 50 teachers employed in Fethullah Gülen's schools in Russia have been deported during the past year for activities inimical to the national interests of Russia. From 2001 to 2006, the number of schools closed reached 16. Furthermore, in 2003, ten teachers employed in Gülen's schools in the autonomous Republic of Başkurdistan were expelled and deported.

During his official visit to Turkey in 2004 President Putin is reported to have expressed his government's displeasure about the activities of these schools by accusing them of training elements for participation in various religious organizations and terrorist groups.

Following the publication, in the European media, of some offending cartoons, Fethullah Gülen couldn't pass up on the opportunity to settle some old scores with his old enemy, the Kemalist/Secular Republic:

> It would be hard to refute the Danes, the French and others, if they, now, would turn around and say to us: "In the past, hasn't the Koran been labeled in your papers a desert law? Wasn't HE called the prophet of the Arab? And haven't you, in a sense, considered the act of deliverance from HIM an act of human emancipation?" Indeed even today there are those who continue to show their disrespect for HIM.

A transcript of the whole interview was published in *Zaman*, February 8 and 9, 2006. The audio of the interview was accessible through www.herkul.org/bamteli.

◆   ◆   ◆

The University of Van has been, for some time, the battleground between two opposing concepts of what the future of the republic ought to be. Until the election of President Yücel Aşkın and his staff, the University was under the influence of reactionary forces, dominated mostly by religious orders—nakşibendi and nurcu—and the followers of a few sheiks and religious figures.

Following a thorough housecleaning by the new president, the reform-minded forces were in the ascendancy. However, in the aftermath of the last general elections and the arrival of an Islamist government, the tables have been turned against the reformers. The minister of national education, Hüseyin Çelik, is a native of Van. His brother is the secretary of the faculty in the College of Medicine, where a strong Nurcu movement exists.

Van has always been the home of reactionary religious movements. Indeed, the founder of the Nurcu movement, Said Nursi, was a native of the region.

About a century ago, in 1907, he petitioned Sultan Abdülhamid for permission to establish an institution of higher learning (Medrese-ü-Zehra) where Islamic studies as well as scientific disciplines would be taught. Having failed to secure the blessing of the sultan, he returned empty handed and left his wishes as a testament to his followers.

When the Republican regime laid the foundations of a modern-day university in Van in 1982 (on the one hundredth anniversary of the birth of Atatürk), the Nurcu movement immediately seized the occasion and tried to hijack the project. A battle for the hearts and minds of the citizenry has been waged ever since. The current chairman of the Department of Pediatrics, Prof. Dursun Odabaş, along with nineteen other faculty members, under the guise of religious freedom, joined nationwide demonstrations organized by the advocates of Sharia laws on October 11, 1998. He was then the dean of the College of Medicine. All nineteen agitators were dismissed from their faculty positions. However, they were allowed to return by court order.

The religious faction within the university has since developed strong links with various religious groups active in and around Van. The 2002 elections were the final chapter in this long saga.

By the end of 2005 President Yücel Aşkın was facing trumped-up charges related to equipment purchases carried out during the term of his predecessor. Handcuffed and sent to jail for almost seventy-five days, he was paying the price for trying to keep the Nur-Zehra-Hizbullah coalition from seizing control of the institution and converting it to what they call the "Madrasa of Zehra," or Medrese-ü-Zehra, which they have been attempting to do for some time. In fact, in 1990, the Nurcu movement formed a foundation called Zehra Foundation for Education and Culture, with the explicit goal of establishing the Medrese-ü-Zehra.

Meanwhile in Ankara, in a joint communiqué, all seventy presidents of the state universities stood behind the embattled President Yücel Aşkın, declaring their total solidarity with him, questioning the legality of the process, and accusing the government of attempting to make the University look more like a *madrasa*.

But the reactionary forces were now coming out into the open, challenging the secular republic in terms that would have been unthinkable just a few years earlier. As is the usual practice in the Middle East, the mob, calling themselves "Muslim students," were now threatening the dean of the College of Agriculture for having closed the prayer room within the college. The warning read, "Atheist Dog, first your wife, and then you will pay the ultimate price." The flyers were signed, "Hizbullah. Allah-u Ekber." A vice-president of the university, according to media reports, moved around campus surrounded by bodyguards.

For over two months, President Aşkın has been subjected to an inhumane form of political lynching. Denied due process and kept literally incommunicado for almost a month, he suffered from severe sleep deprivation and mental torture thought to occur only in the most vicious police states. Now, one might be justified to ask, where were the human rights "commissars" of the EU? After all, year after year, they have harassed the Turkish governments for the mistreatment of other citizens, and rightly so. But now they seem to have vanished. Apparently, intervention on behalf of victims of torture has to be selective and meet certain criteria not found among the Copenhagen ones.

There is another angle to this episode. In the course of the judicial inquiry that was carried out it became apparent that the Turkish justice system has become another victim of the confrontation between the reactionaries and the reformers.

◆   ◆   ◆

October 2005 saw yet another issue symptomatic of the Islamist regime's obsession with the symbols of Islam. The city council and the mayor of Greater Istanbul approved the building of a mosque within a park located in the village of Göztepe, a suburb of Istanbul. There was a problem, however: the local mayor insisted that his community needed the park more than the mosque, since there were plenty of mosques, some even close to the proposed location. But the Islamist Municipality of Greater Istanbul ignored his plea, and as of this writing, the mosque will be constructed.

It is not uncommon for religious fervor to seize elected officials who wish to cash in on the votes of the faithful. The promise of returning the Saint Sophia to its previous status as a mosque has always been a favorite of reactionary politicians. As a mayor, Prime Minister Recep Tayyip Erdoğan resorted to a similar gimmick by promising to build a mosque right at the edge of Taksim Square in the European district of Istanbul.

Today, the number of communities where it is practically impossible to run into billboards with swimsuits is greater than it was just a few years ago. In the heartland of Anatolia, several municipalities have forbidden the serving of alcohol. The AKP-dominated Municipality of Greater Ankara does not allow the sale of alcohol at its many recreational sites, including Lake Mogan.

In many cities, men and women are to use separate public beaches and transportation services. And now, the Islamist movement is about to embark on the most devastating assault upon the national secular education system: a draft bill under consideration by the government will make the private education system an equal partner with the nationwide public education system. The result of this free market solution to the nation's education problems will be to enrich the private school "operators" while at the same time facilitate the indoctrination of youth into the ways of radical Islam. In fact, Turkey's greatest misfortune has been the convergence of a fundamentalist religious movement with a savage *laissez faire/laissez passer* economic policy, which has left millions unemployed and below the poverty threshold. The same political cadre is responsible for both trends.

Max Thornburg, a former executive of Standard Oil, wrote in 1949, "The impression that one carries from Turkey is that of a thin layer of modernity imported from abroad and imposed from above, with great will and vigor, upon a population the larger part of which is still steeped in medieval or even ancient ways of life."

In the half-century following this statement, the western part of Anatolia—certainly its major cities, Istanbul, Ankara, Izmir—and the touristic littoral along the Mediterranean sea, may have changed markedly, but unfortunately the same cannot be said of the eastern part of the land. Thirty years later, in 1980, the American anthropologist Carol Delaney, who spent two years studying a Central Anatolian village, found that village life had changed little, both culturally and economically—it was still centered on procreation and rigid gender roles.

Nevertheless, the publication of a report (Islamic Calvinism: Change and Conservatism in Central Anatolia, *European Stability Initiative,* September 19, 2005) likening Muslim capitalist businesses of Central Anatolia to the Calvinist movement of Christianity, at first generated very little reaction. Its claim that Central Anatolian businessmen identify Calvinism and the Protestant work ethic as a most appropriate way of describing their approach to business, and that individualistic, pro-business currents have become increasingly prominent within Turkish Islam, were unusual and hard to verify.

Some liberal voices began expressing serious reservations. Özdemir Ince and Fatih Altaylı come to mind. They viewed the main thrust of the report as a naked attempt to come up with a concept of Islam acceptable to the "dominant Christian culture." Özdemir Ince went one step further and saw in all this the hidden hand of those who advocate Turkish participation in the famous (or infamous) U.S. State Department's Middle East Partnership Initiative (MEPI). Indeed, the report identifies the Nakşibendi, Nurcu, and Fethullahcı movements of Islam as the main engines of the industrialization program in Turkey, which makes the report's conclusions rather suspect and self-serving. In all likelihood, the report was prepared with funds provided by the three religious movements in concert with the Central Intelligence Agency. The recent charges leveled against the Fethullahcı schools in Russia of collaborating with CIA had caused many to wonder how these organizations amass their resources.

But all that mild reaction changed when Ertuğrul Özkök (*Hürriyet*, January 26, 2006) pointed to Fethullah Gülen as the potential Calvin of Turkey. After this, all hell broke loose. Some writers from the religious right seemed on the verge of apoplexy. (Ali Bulac, 'Islam Kalvinistleri', *Zaman* January 27, 2006; Yaşar Taşkın Koç, 'Yeni Islam'da neyin nesi?', *8Sütun.com*, January 26, 2006; Mustafa Özel, 'Islam, Protestanlık ve Kapitalizm' *Yeni Şafak* January 22, 29, 2006*)*.

But the voice of the religious right, the daily *Zaman*, had the last word.
It carried (January 26, 2006) an immediate disclaimer from none other than Fethullah Gülen himself:

> I am a regular Moslem who is respectful of all aspects of the faith, within the framework of the Koran, of the Prophet's own words, and of the consensus of opinion of all religious scholars. Any attempt to consider changing any issue related to the Faith, including the rules of behavior within Islam, in my view, is forbidden and is the biggest sin. I would prefer to die a thousand times rather than change any aspect of the Faith, even those concerning the rules of behavior. I am neither a Calvinist nor a reformist. All my life, I have not made any such claim nor have I intimated at such. In my opinion, today, what needs reformation is not the faith, but rather our piety. As I have expressed on many occasions many times over, I am a simple, modest Moslem, bound, and bound rather solidly, by tradition, and marching along the path of a glorious Faith.

So much for Fethullah the Calvinist! It is not clear if this was a tempest in a tea cup or not. The swiftness with which the message was delivered indicated that the Turkish Ayatollah was is no mood to approve an Islamic reformation. One interesting aspect of this exchange was that the disclaimer was not posted on Fethullah Gülen's Web site.

The furious reaction generated in the Islamist media when a woman—who happened to be the wife of an advisor to RTE—took part in a Friday prayer and stood in a mosque, with her uncovered hair, next to men, was no less spectacular. It was characteristic of the fundamentalist nature of the supporters of the regime. To prevent a repeat performance during the following Friday's prayer, none other than the local head of the Religious Affairs Directorate was waiting, with scarves on hand!

All that brings to mind Reinhold Niebuhr, the most influential American theologian of the twentieth century, who reminded his fellow citizens, "Religion is so frequently a source of confusion in political life, and so frequently dangerous to democracy, precisely because it introduces absolutes into the realm of relative values."

◆   ◆   ◆

So the critical question we are faced with today concerns the future course the nation will take. Will it move towards a modern, secular republic representing a prosperous free society, or will it take a turn to the right and end up as a reactionary, religious "second Republic?" By administering a simple litmus test one can determine the direction in which *this* administration is headed:

- If an administration undermines the educational standards adopted since the early years of the republic in order to open the way to private religious curriculum in elementary schools;

- if it continues building mosques even though there are far more mosques than schools;

- if it introduces the separation of the sexes (*harem-selamlık*) in public places, including swimming pools, movie theaters, busses, and beaches;

- if it focuses more on the "headscarf" than the issue of education of girls;

- if it bends the rules and facilitates the opening of religious schools without requiring their certification;

- if it condones officials ordering the covering of advertisement panels displaying scantily attired women;

- if the local religious authority in the Department of Çorum/Iskilip can issue a religious opinion that leads to the removal of public urinals on the ground that it is not in accord with the teaching of the Koran;

- if officials can order the removal, from a public square, of a monument found to have legs that are too naked;

- if it can order separate service hours and/or locations for the sexes at every social establishment in a community;

- if the radio-television services can decides to replace the prayer read in Turkish during the breaking of the fast with a reading—in Arabic—of the ninety-nine names of Allah;

- if a controversially appointed chief physician at a state hospital orders the conversion of a toilet room into a prayer room in the name of "increased quality of service" offered to patients;

- if the ministry of national education can propose a revised religious studies curriculum for high schools requiring the learning, among other topics, of the rules regarding the "ritual of ablution";

- if students at Yalova Atatürk (oh the irony!) Primary school, as part of their weekly religious studies curriculum, are taken to the mosque next door for the demonstration of the rituals of prayers;

- if at another primary school (Mecidiyeköy), the *müezzin*, who is in the state's employ, is hired and assigned as instructor of religious studies and promptly takes the class to his mosque for hands-on teaching (*Cumhuriyet*, December 2, 2005);

- if the highest religious authority, in a sermon/prayer read throughout the nation's mosques (March 11, 2005) can openly advocate discrimination against non-believers as well as non-Muslims;

- if the radio-television directorate can bar all contemporary and Republican choirs from performing during all programs celebrating Moslim-feasts (Kandil) and assigns choir duties only to groups associated with the "Nurcu" movement;

- if an elected municipal council and its mayor (Denizli) can vote to move all liquor-serving establishments outside the city limits;

- if an administration's highest office holder (RTE) can order separate prayer rooms (*mescit*) for the sexes within the offices of the prime ministry;

- if the director of national education (for the Province of Konya) can circulate to all female teachers within the province a dress code stressing the importance of not provoking erotic feelings among male students by wearing tight pants;

- if the director of national education (for the Province of Mersin) can equate the teaching of evolution to the undermining of the students' religious beliefs and attempt to fire teachers on such grounds;

- if the minister of national education is the same person who, during the 2001 budget debates, opposed the eight years of compulsory education as destructive for the future of the feeder schools that support the *imam-hatip* education;

- if the minister of national education insists on appointing to key posts personnel identified as unsuitable because of their anti-secular activities;

- if the minister of national education does not hesitate to appoint as a provincial director of national education a man who has spent time in jail for favoritism towards a religious fanatic (Karases Cemalettin Kaplan);

- if the minister of national education attempts to place his religious cronies at key posts in the ministry by dismissing over five hundred of the ministry's personnel but is rebuffed by the courts, who return most of them to their previous positions;

- if the ministry of national education approves the adoption of a book declaring all institutions of the Turkish Republic to be despicable, and another book claiming any educational system not focusing on the study of the Koran to be responsible for the development of troubled and dysfunctional juveniles;

- if textbooks where M. Kemal's mother has her hair uncovered are now revised and the picture is being replaced with one where she has her head covered;

- if female members of the ruling party attending the annual convention (in the province of Kars) had to be seated behind walls of curtain separating them from the male audience;

- if for the highest religious authority, the directorate of religious affairs, having a photo taken with uncovered hair is a sin and women should use, if necessary, a wig to make sure the real hair is not visible;

- if a regime's local party leader (in the province of Afyon) refuses to shake the hand of women for religious reasons;

- if the first line of defense against the avian flu is to ask the *imams* to read a *hutbe* from the pulpit during the Friday sermon warning against the risks of handling feathered birds;

- if the neurology department of a university (Pamukkale) hospital cannot find space to accommodate an intensive care unit but will designate two separate prayer rooms, one for each sex;

- if an administration's choice to head the Turkish Central Bank is a crony for whom 'charging interest' is immoral;

- if an administration is represented in Parliament by an MP who seeks official assurance that the toothbrush he is using doesn't contain swine hair;

- if parliamentarians of the majority party, after devoting several hours of deliberations to the issue of women praying with uncovered hair and side by side with men, are unable to conclude whether the practice is an abomination (*mekruh*) or not;

- if the prime minister's secretary of state can declare the republic "out of fashion" and emphasize the need to redefine secularism, nationalism, and republicanism using religious formulations;

- In short, if an administration condones a perverted religious zealotry combined with a good dose of anti-modernism and intolerance, one can safely assume that this is not a secular administration but rather one that is sliding inexorably into the abyss of radical Islam!

Yet, most people familiar with the teaching of Islam would readily acknowledge that the actions above are the consequences of a corrupt interpretation of the faith. In the words of Reinhold Niebuhr: "The worst corruption is the corruption of a religion."

As for the prime minister, he finally placed an exclamation point on his interpretation of how to approach the hot issue of the headscarf. During a visit to Copenhagen, Denmark, on November 15, 2005, he reacted to the verdict of the European high court for human rights. The court had declared earlier that the ban of the headscarf in universities was legitimate action. Erdoğan, reacting rather strongly to the verdict, sounded for the first time since taking office like a man who longed for the days of the Sharia rule. Indeed, by declaring the court incompetent on the issue of headscarf and insisting that only the learned men of Muslim theology (*ulema*) can decide on issues pertaining to religious practices, he brought to mind several questions he will have to answer: What else should the *ulema* be consulted about? The practice of polygamy? The inheritance rights of women vs. men? The appropriateness of stoning as a form of capital punishment? And whose *ulema* should render judgment? The ayatollahs of Shia Islam or the high priests of the Wahabi sect of Sunni Islam?

◆   ◆   ◆

A final piece of the puzzle emerged with the visit to Ankara of Halid Meşal, the leader of the political wing of the Palestinian movement Hamas. The government, unable to admit the inherent contradiction of meeting with the leader of a group they have publicly declared a terrorist organization, attempted to hide behind a completely disingenuous defense: it was the party (AKP), not the government, that was host to the Hamas leader, and the PM did not meet with him. That the issue was discussed and debated at the ministerial council before a decision to issue a visa was taken and that Vice-Premier and Minister of Foreign Affairs Abdullah Gül did eventually meet Meşal at the AKP headquarters, were for the Islamist Government, trivial details not worth discussing.

The end result of such a duplicitous foreign policy, equivalent to the religious practice called *takiyye*, can lead to only one outcome: a Turkey mistrusted by all and respected by a few. The administration is grossly mistaken if it believes that it can placate its Islamist base by appeasement. This will only encourage them to ask for more.

Following the publication of the caricatures of the Prophet Mohammed in a Danish newspaper, Recep Tayyip Erdoğan and Jose Louis Rodriguez Zapatero, prime ministers of Turkey and Spain respectively, jointly penned an open letter in which they called for "maximum respect for…beliefs," adding that "there are no rights without responsibility and respect for different sensibilities…" They concluded that the publication of these caricatures—even if legal—is not indifferent and thus ought to be rejected from a moral and political standpoint. ("A Call for Respect and Calm," *International Herald Tribune*, 5 February 2006.)

Now, it is highly revealing to compare the views expressed above with the manifesto issued by a dozen writers—Salman Rushdie, Ayaan Hirsi Ali, Taslima Nasreen, Bernard-Henri Levy, Chahla Chafiq, Irshad Manji, Mehdi Mozaffari, Maryam Namazie, Ibn Warraq, Caroline Fourest, Antoine Sfeir, and Philippe Val—who have had their share of difficulties with Islamic militancy in the past. In fact, two of them—Rushdie and Nasreen—have had *fatwa*s issued ordering their execution. Their manifesto declares "Islamism" as the next global threat the world is facing. Refuting the concept of a "clash of civilization," they assert that "we are witnessing a global struggle confronting democrats and theocrats." In a ringing defense of secular values, the manifesto adds that, nurtured by fears and frustrations, Islamism is a reactionary ideology that kills equality, freedom, and secularism wherever it is present. (*Charlie Hebdo*, March 1, 2006)

The contrast between these two divergent points of view should help Turkish Islamists appreciate the depth of the misgivings they generate with regard their sincerity vis à vis secularism and the place of women in their social model.

3

A SHACKLED SOVEREIGNTY

High above the speaker's chair, it is written in bold letters, "Sovereignty belongs unconditionally to the nation!" The chamber of deputies in the Turkish Parliament has displayed this motto ever since Kemal Atatürk led the Turkish nation to victory in the war of liberation. The notion of unconditional sovereignty has been with the Turkish people ever since, even though, from time to time, activities not in the best interest of the nation and injurious to its sovereignty have been recognized as part of the nation's realpolitik. Here is the real question: at what point does a considered sacrifice based on the best available data becomes surrender, and when does surrender become dishonorable and abject? No one will question the fact that by associating itself with NATO, Turkey agreed to follow certain policies that have limited its freedom of action. But when considering the aftermath of the Cyprus intervention, one observes that the reactions were generally from state to state. When on July 15, 1974 a Greek military junta in Athens staged a coup in Cyprus and ousted its Greek-Cypriot leader, Archbishop Makarios, Turkey, as one of the three guarantor states—along with Britain and Greece-had intervened and occupied the northern third of the island. NATO as a defensive alliance did not, at the time, take a position. However, the United States, influenced by a strong Greek lobby in Congress, took unilateral action by imposing an arms embargo. Furthermore, President Johnson, in a letter to then Prime Minister Ecevit, threatened to ignore United States' alliance obligations to come to Turkey's aid should the Soviet Union intervened militarily. This sort of intervention (resorting to some form of economic or military trade pressure) also marked the ten years of low-intensity warfare raging in the southeast of Turkey against the PKK terrorist organization. The West German decision to deny the sale of Leopard tanks to the Turkish army was a case in point.

Evidently, no candid discussion of Turkish foreign policy could neglect to address the role of the European Union in imposing on Turkey, in addition to its "admission criteria for membership" and the well known Copenhagen Criteria, certain conditions that a truly independent country would find unacceptable, even insulting. Similarly, the United States' efforts to hire Turkey's services to convert the Middle Eastern theocracies and autocracies into democratic "moderate" Islamic states are equally objectionable. More recently, the Turkish media reported that during his visit to the White House, Prime Minister Erdoğan was confronted with a set of so-called Washington Criteria to be used to determine how sincere the Prime Minister was when addressing his American interlocutors. Apparently, the litmus test will be to see how loud and clear he is when he addresses, before domestic audiences, the positions he holds abroad.

◆   ◆   ◆

So, how sovereign is Turkey? International relations are usually affected by either military or financial equations, or a combination thereof. The examples offered above were of the first kind. A less appreciated danger is when a country's financial health is in jeopardy and the enemies are eager to take advantage of it.

How does one then assess Turkey's sovereignty from a financial point of view?

An astute observer of the Turkish financial sector, writer, scholar, and expert commentator Yiğit Bulut, in an article titled "Is Turkey Sovereign?" (*Radikal*, 21 January 2005), addressed the issue head on. According to Bulut, the dynamics upon which Turkish economy has been built depends upon consumption-led growth, an influx of hot money, and the systematic practice of constant borrowing in order to defer debt payments.

However, in countries considered to be competing in the same league with Turkey, the situation is quite different. Their economic program rests on the three pillars of production-led growth, debt consolidation, and direct capital influx rather than borrowing.

Yiğit Bulut traces the origin of Turkey's present dilemma to January 1978 and points the finger at a report prepared by Kemal Derviş and Sherman Robinson for the World Bank, in which they made a series of recommendations. While no elected government was willing to heed them, they were immediately adopted following the military coup of 1980 and, as a result, what had been until 1978 a successful economic and financial model, based on production growth and small-scale individual capital formations, has been reduced into a large-scale free market driven by multinationals. It was also the beginning of large-scale capital flight.

According to Yiğit Bulut, the conditions went from bad to worse. During the post 1980 era, the national debt which was almost "nil" kept ballooning and has now reached $300 billion. Currently 40–50 percent of the national budget is being, annually, allocated to the service of the debt. Bulut's unforgiven and most alarming conclusion is a harsh indictment of the political elite who has been running the show for quite some time: "Turkey is now the only place where blood-thirsty investors can earn a pleasant retun for their money. Give a loan, and earn, on a dollar basis, more than 10 percent and relax…Final word: My beautiful country, which spends over $1 billion in interest payments, please wake up!"

The situation described above is eerily similar to the sequence of events that unfolded in 1875. Foreign investor interest was at a peak, since the interest yield from the Ottoman treasury was twice as high as on most English investments. Very few realized that the interest, as it accrued, was paid by the Turks not out of increasing state revenues but out of further foreign loans and bond issues. The bottom line: Turkey was borrowing all the money she needed to pay the interest. Within twenty years, the Ottoman debt rose from four million to two hundred million pounds.

The ballooning charges on the debt began to absorb more than 50 percent of the Ottoman government's annual resources. In the words of Lord Kinross (*The Ottoman Centuries,* 1977), "Economic catastrophe began to loom large."

◆   ◆   ◆

It is important to know some of the actors who took center stage following the 1980 military coup. Kenan Evren, the chief of general staff responsible for the coup, has always been, and still is, an avid advocate of the Turk-Islam synthesis. The general responsible for the torture and execution of many young leftists, he became the first president to visit Mecca for the pilgrimage. He forced Parliament to adopt a constitution where secularism coexisted, believe it or not, with an article that made it compulsory the teaching of Islam in schools. He was responsible for the state's ill-advised policy of building mosques in Alevi villages, even though Alevis do not attend or pray in mosques. And he and the junta that grabbed power along with him is said to have had the support of the United States. It was reported that they were referred to as "our boys" in the halls of the Pentagon.

But Kenan Evren will certainly be remembered more for an unintended consequence of his actions: the landslide election victory by the Motherland Party, led by Turgut Özal. Indeed, the Motherland Party's rule over the Turkish political scene was a watershed epoch in which Turkey began to discover the intoxicating pleasure of borrowing. And Turkey, once in the clutches of the international lending agencies, never again regained control of the levers of sovereign government. In fact, over the years, Turkey has continuously borrowed from IMF, World Bank, Bank of International Development, and others. She has currently the dubious distinction of being one of the nations most indebted to the IMF.

As for Turgut Özal, the darling of the rich and powerful business community, he was assured a vice-premiership in the post-coup government after Vehbi Koç, one of the wealthiest men in Turkey and a member of the old guard business elite interceded with Kenan Evren. Such relationships have become more and more routine with every new regime.

In addition to international borrowing, and ever since the eighties, the government, in order to meet its budget obligations, has engaged in an orgy of internal borrowing. Worst of all, high interest rate policies over the past twenty-five years have invited a horde of hot—speculative money which, at the first sign of economic downturn or fiscal impasse, left the country in a hurry leaving behind a trail of financial and banking crises and inevitable devaluations. The "borrowing to pay back old debts" days of the Ottoman era were here again. The practice became the principal fiscal instrument of successive Turkish governments. The situation today is far more serious given the fact that the international lending agencies now have virtual veto power over the government's budget expenditures, as they insist that a budget surplus (after interest repayments) of at least 6.5 percent be achieved and directed towards the repayment of outstanding debts.

When a country devotes 50 percent of its annual budget to pay interest on its debt, it stands to reason that it can not direct many funds towards the normal areas of responsibility of a "sovereign" government. Today's Turkish budget devotes less than 3 percent towards national health, about 10 percent towards education, and less than 4 percent towards national defense. And yet Turkey's internal debt, which hovered around $65 billions just three years ago, is now over $150 billion and rising. The need to ask the nation to make some serious sacrifices is clear, but the will to face the nation honestly has never been this government's (or any previous one's) strong suit. With nearly half of the economy operating underground, indirect taxes have become a crushing burden on the middle and working classes. Today, Europe's most expensive gasoline is sold in Turkey.

Living on the edge, facing one imminent financial crisis after another, Turkey has so far managed to postpone the day of reconing solely because international capital expects Turkey to be gradually but eventually absorbed into the market economy of the European Union. The assumption is that the prospect of Turkey's EU membership will open up great opportunities to acquire most, if not all, of Turkey's major infrastructures, including its ports, refineries, steel mills, cement factories, power plants, not to mention the potential inroads into her consumer market. One needs only to read the daily papers to realize that such a day is already upon us. All the great and proud achievements of the Kemalist past are on the "privatization" block.

◆   ◆   ◆

There are other areas where Turkish national interests are being threatened by external forces working in tandem with their local collaborators. But in these areas too, the Islamist regime's survival instinct dictates measures capable of jeopardizing the future of a "sovereign" state. The problem of Cyprus; the relationship with Armenia (including European pressure on Turkey to recognize the consequences of the forced evacuation of hundreds of thousand of Armenians from the eastern front during WWI as genocide); European pressure to recognize Kurds and Alevis as legitimate minorities within the Turkish constitutional framework; Greece's territorial claims to certain islets on the Aegean sea; and the demand that Turkey recognize the ecclesiastical title of "ecumenical" of the Greek Orthodox Church situated in Fener, Istanbul, and allow the opening of its Heybeliada (Chalki) Greek Orthodox seminary are all sensitive issues. In most of these cases, yielding to international pressure seems to be the price this government will have to pay in order to achieve accession into the EU. How can a regime willing to pay any price in order to get through the door of the EU still claim to be "sovereign?"

Now that Turkey has been given the green light to begin "open-ended" negotiations, the realistic goal of which is a "virtual" membership, the Turkish-European Union relationship has entered uncharted territory. The humiliations, insults, and indignities suffered by this proud nation during the past few years could fill volumes. The "Opening Statement and the "Negotiating Framework" document adopted on October 3, 2005, by the Council of the European Union during the Accession Conference with Turkey is full of traps ready to be triggered as excuses to deny Turkey full membership. Article 2 of the Negotiating Framework states,

> These negotiations are an open-ended process, the outcome of which cannot be guaranteed beforehand. While having full regard to all Copenhagen criteria, including the absorption capacity of the Union, if Turkey is not in a posi-

tion to assume in full all the obligations of membership it must be ensured that Turkey is fully anchored in the European structures through the strongest possible bond.

In other words, the EU has, for all practical purposes, presented a subtle version of the infamous "privileged partnership" status.

The Islamist government is fully aware of the ignominious nature of this partnership, so much so that it is reluctant to submit the Additional Protocol extending the Association Agreement to all new EU member states—including the Republic of Cyprus—to the Turkish Parliament for ratification. In fact, a former Prime Minister, Mesut Yılmaz, predicted a deadlock during the accession talks if and when the deliberations touch upon the subject of Cyprus. Many political commentators and analysts acknowledge the near impossibility for any political party to acquiesce to the kind of solution dictated in the EU Negotiating Framework given the fact that Article 10 requires Turkey to apply the *acquis* of the Union, including "acts, legally binding or not, adopted within the Union framework, such as inter-institutional agreements, resolutions, statements, recommendations, guidelines…"

◆   ◆   ◆

One such inter-institutional resolution, almost concurrently adopted by the EU Parliament, clearly highlights the "game plan." On September 29, 2005, the European Parliament adopted a resolution on the opening of negotiations with Turkey. Article 3 of the resolution

> …reminds Turkey that by maintaining restrictions against vessels flying the Cypriot flag…by denying them access to Turkish ports, and against Cypriot aircraft, and by denying them overflight rights and landing rights at Turkish airports, Turkey is in breach of the Ankara Agreement and the related Customs Union, irrespective of the Protocol, and this practice infringes the principle of the free movement of goods; calls, therefore, on Turkey fully to implement all the provisions of the Protocol.

Then, in Article 4, the trap is set:

> Call on the Commission to make, by the end of 2006, a full assessment of the implementation of the extended Ankara Agreement, and stresses that failure in the implementation of this agreement will have serious implications for the

negotiation process and could even lead to a halting of the negotiation process; demands, therefore, that the implementation of the Customs Union be amongst the first chapters to be dealt with in the accession negotiations in 2006.

And if the above is insufficient to block the process (or to humiliate), there is always Article 6, which

> emphasizes that a rapid normalization of relations between Turkey and all EU Member States, including Turkey's recognition of the Republic of Cyprus, is a necessary component of the accession process; stresses that Turkey's recognition of the Republic of Cyprus can in no way be the subject of the negotiations; calls on the Turkish authorities to normalize relations between Turkey and all EU Member States and recognize the Republic of Cyprus as soon as possible, and stresses that failure to do so will have serious implications for the negotiation process and could even lead to a halting of the negotiation process.

In adopting the following amendments, the EU Parliament proved itself capable of rubbing salt to Turkish wounds and in the process making the accession even more problematic:

> Paragraph 1. ...the EU Parliament notes that the commission and the council take the view that Turkey has formally fulfilled the final conditions for starting the accession negotiations on 3 October 2005.

> It is of the opinion that, on these and other points, the implementation still has to be fulfilled.

> Paragraph 3a. ...the EU Parliament calls on Turkey to recognize the Armenian genocide and considers this recognition a prerequisite for accession to the European Union.

Just as appalling is the blunt nature of Articles 14 and 15 of the resolution adopted by the EU Parliament. It reminds Turkey that "permanent safeguards for the free movement of workers" will have to be considered and that "accession is thus not the automatic consequence of the start of the negotiations."

The Islamist government, true to form, affixed its signature on this document fully cognizant of the fact that it can never deliver on these articles. But to begin the accession negotiations—regardless of the cost—has always been this regime's only realistic survival plan. The cost of this abject surrender to every wish of EU member states will be heavy indeed.

As for the European leaders, by engaging Turkey in an open-ended negotiation process, they were taking some risks on their own home fronts. The rejection by French and Dutch voters of the European Union Charter was blamed on their reluctance to admit Turkey into the Union. The media were scathing in their comments:

> Let us summarize. In their majority, the Europeans do not desire a marriage with Turkey. They intend, in effect, to preserve their culture. The French said it on May 29 by rejecting a Union without border. They confirmed it when they responded to polls. The poll by Sofres, reported Monday, indicates that 42 percent (versus 26 percent) of them believe that their identity is being threatened rather then protected by Brussels. It is not possible to be more explicit. That is the reason why the engagements with Ankara, imposed Monday by the Twenty-Five, are an insult to democracy. (Ivan Rioufol, *Le Figaro*, 7 October 2005)

Another influential European was just as harsh in his remarks. Alan Lamassoure, European MP and national secretary for European affairs of France's right-wing UMP party, had this to say:

> To say that a country 95 percent of whose territory is situated in Asia Minor is "European" is to admit, implicitly, that the European Union has no borders. Indeed, tomorrow, how will we refuse admission to Russia, Armenia, the countries of the Caucasus, Israel, and the future state of Palestine—followed by other "Mediterranean" states?

He further asserted that the only option remaining is for the EU to offer Turkey a regime of privileged partnership. Accusing the European leaders of making promises to Turkey that they are, today, unable to deliver, Lamassoure predicts a climate of mutual mistrust which, he believes, will become more poisonous at each stage of the negotiations. He concludes:

> The unquestionable truth is that, since the major crisis of the last Spring, the European Union has neither the institutions, nor the budget, nor the public support that would be essential to render credible an offer of accession to Turkey. In the absence of such a language of truth, October 3 will remain the day of fools. Let us have the courage to propose to the Turks a new regime of privileged partnership. (Alain Lamassoure, *Le Figaro*, 1 October 2005)

These comments merit serious consideration by Turkish government officials who, at this time, are sitting at the table waiting for the next shoe to drop. Realistically, Turkey has been put on notice that the best she can hope for is an eviscerated membership status with none of the privileges accorded to member states. Even the much sought after development funds awarded to developing sectors and regions of new members will be very little when compared to those offered to Portugal, Spain, and Greece.

◆   ◆   ◆

A more ominous development in Turkey's European aspiration and candidacy is the tone and the nature of the condemnation coming from across the Atlantic. Just about the time when Turkey was hoping to begin the long and arduous journey toward "membership," some old friends were sounding alarm bells. In the United States, the liberal media has always been Turkey's Achilles heel. Powerful lobbies of Greek-, Armenian-, and even Kurdish-American interests have always been active in the halls of Congress against the interests of Turkey. But the conservatives, mainly Republicans, were reliable in their support. Lately, liberal influential Jewish lobbies, appreciative of past Turkish policies of an even-handed approach to the Israeli-Palestinian conflict, had joined forces with the neo-conservatives in promoting policies supportive of Turkey. Moreover, following the success of the AKP in the 2002 general elections, Prime Minister Recep Tayyip Erdoğan became, overnight, the darling of the White House and the American administration. He was looked upon as a role model and a useful instrument in achieving the goals of President Bush's "Great Middle East Project," through which democracy was supposed to be transplanted throughout the Islamic World.

Good and friendly relations with the United States have always been a cornerstone of Turkish foreign policy. Yet this regime, in the course of three short years, seems to have wrecked the foundations of this "special relationship." The reasons can easily be discerned by carefully examining articles that have appeared recently in the US media.

On February 16, 2005, in an article titled "The Sick Man of Europe—Again," Robert L. Pollock, a senior editorial page writer of the *Wall Street Journal*, analyzed the causes of the rise of anti-American madness in Turkey. Describing the present regime as "subtle yet insidious Islamism of the Justice and Development (AK) Party" Pollock points the finger at a "combination of old leftism and new Islamism" to explain the collapse in Turkish-American relations. He concludes that if a few more years of "riding the tiger" continues, "much of Atatürk's legacy risks being lost, and there won't be any of the old Ottoman grandeur left, either. Turkey could easily become just another second-rate country: small-minded, paranoid, marginal and—how could it be otherwise?—friendless in America and unwelcome in Europe."

The above broadside was followed by a couple of articles with questionable objectives written by Michael Rubin (*National Review Online*, August 2, 2005, and *Haaretz*, September 30, 2005). They had very little to do with Turkey's accession to the EU but a lot to do with defending the interests of a certain aggrieved businessman, Mustafa Süzer, whose shady deals and corrupt business practices had led him into hot water with the law. Rubin's attempt to pressure the administration and get something for his business friends will be examined in Chapter 5, when surveying the conglomerate-controlled Turkish media and its incestuous relations with the regime.

The heaviest blow against Erdoğan and the AKP came during the EU-Turkey accession negotiations. A well known neo-con, Frank J. Gaffney Jr., president of the Center for Security Policy, a conservative Washington think tank, in a column for the *Washington Times* (September 27, 2005), said, "'No' to Islamist Turkey."

The reason: "Prime Minister Erdoğan is systematically turning his country from a secular democracy into an Islamofascist state governed by an ideology anathema to European values and freedoms." As evidence for such an "ominous transformation" Gaffney points to the fact that Saudi Arabian and Persian Gulf State funds withdrawn from the United States after September 11, 2001 are now flooding the Turkish capital market. He underlined the possibility that this unaccountable cash is being laundered in Turkey to be used to finance Islamofascist terrorism.

Turning his attention to the secular educational system, Gaffney remarks that it is being steadily supplanted by "imam-hatip" schools where students are taught the Islamofascist interpretation of the Koran. Gaffney further observes that Erdoğan's AKP Party is currently engaged in a systematic replacement of secular bureaucrats with religious cronies or "theo-apparatchicks" and in packing the courts as a precursor to the days of Sharia. The exclamation point in Gafney's analysis is as blunt as it gets: "As elsewhere, religious intolerance is hallmark of Mr. Erdogan's creeping Islamofascist *putsch* in Turkey."

Some other arguments offered by Gaffney are stangely reminiscent of Michael Rubin's defense of some corrupt businessmen. The Islamization, undoubtedly, is a clear and present danger for the secular republic, and Frank Gaffney's arguments highlighting the risk were right on the mark. However, the ravages inflicted on the Turkish economy by corrupt businessmen who, in cahoots with their international partners, have shamelessly attacked and ransacked the national treasury can't be underestimated. If anything, the regime's forgiving attitude towards all sorts of ethical lapses by corrupt businessmen is just as serious a threat to the very foundations of the republic as Islamization.

The attacks against the policies of the Islamist regime continued unabated. Michael Rubin, in a couple of articles *(National Review Online,* "Will They or Won't They? The future of Turkey and Europe," October 3, 2005; and "Turkey's No Casual Dining," December 12, 2005) dealt with the government's assault on the rule of law, the attempt to replace professional civil servants with AKP cronies, Erdoğan's disdain for the European High Court for Human Rights' ruling to uphold the headscarf ban in Turkish Universities, the issue of illegal Koran schools, the assault on Turkey's secular traditions, and the prime minister's abuse of power. But he also revisited the same old ground: the government's seizure of Kentbank and Pamukbank and the appeal by Mustafa Süzer, chairman of Kentbank. The motives behind these attacks have generated considerable interest among the Turkish media. We will discuss them later. However, by now, the present Turkish government no longer has the trust and support of the White House. And the neo-con attacks against the regime gained added significance after President G. W. Bush, for the first time, during a speech he delivered on October 6, 2005, at the Ronald Reagan Building and International Trade Center in Washington, D.C., began to substitute the term "Islamic radicalism" for terrorism. Considering that Prime Minister Erdoğan has, on numerous occasions, objected to the use of the terms "Islamic radicals" and "Islamic terrorists," arguing that Islam is a religion of peace, the choice of the term "Islamic radicalism" by the president was a significant departure from earlier rhetoric. Indeed the president has even used the term "Islamofascist," although he attributed it to others who used it to describe certain regimes unfriendly to the U.S.

◆   ◆   ◆

In the past the Turkish-American relationship was a so-called strategic one. Since the arrival of U.S. armed forces next door in Iraq, that relationship has evolved into something quite different. A rather revolutionary point of view was recently expressed by Şükrü Elekdağ, Member of Parliament and former ambassador to Washington. He maintains that the Kurdish terrorist organization PKK has been contracted by the United States to do America's dirty work in and around Iraq. Particularly, he maintained, "the terrorist organization is being used by the U.S. as a pressure weapon against Turkey." Furthermore, he asserted that an independent or autonomous Kurdish state is one of the linchpins of U.S. foreign policy in the Middle East.

Elekdağ states that United States' claim to be too preoccupied in Iraq to take military action against the PKK in Northern Iraq is disingenuous. He claims that the U.S. Army can stop the delivery of any and all logistical supplies overnight, including water and food, and force the surrender of the rebels.

It is too early to predict the outcome. The U.S. may soon find itself facing a familiar question: Who lost Turkey? Turkey is already facing a similar question: Who lost Cyprus? But a more ominous question may soon be on everyone's lips: What went wrong? Whether it is "Islamofascism" or "Moderate Islam" or "Conservative Democracy," as AKP likes to define itself, at the end of the day, Turkey's international standing will depend on how she is perceived with regard to her independent foreign policy.

Which brings us back to the central question of how free and independent Turkish foreign policy can be, given the fact that the present regime's survival depends on its securing the "seal of good housekeeping" of the European Union, the International Monetary Fund, the United States of America and the Green capital of the Middle Eastern theocracies. The government is fully aware that its hope of moving the regime towards a moderate Islam, softly and without generating too many objections among its patrons, cannot be achieved without towing the EU line and the U.S. line, simultaneously if possible. In that respect, accession to the EU has become an obsession with the Islamist regime. The United States too is strongly in favor of anchoring Turkey to the European Union for the simple reason that such an outcome would be the best guaranty against a too independent Turkish foreign policy. And there lies the greatest risk for the republic.

Slowly but inexorably sliding into an unhealthy dependence will lead only to ruination. Ottoman history should have taught the present leaders a few lessons about the consequences of capitulating.

Indeed, in the words of Winston Churchill (Winston Churchill, *The World Crisis: The Aftermath,* 1929) the Ottoman Empire was "loaded with follies, stained with crimes, rotted with misgovernment." And it was this "puppet Government of Turkey" that the "law givers of the world", assembled in Paris in 1919, were dismembering piece by piece, province by province.

Today, Turkey is faced with an enemy who's just as canny, just as merciless, and just as determined to extract a heavy price for allowing its present corrupt and rotten governing regime to survive the consequences of its own misgovernment.

According to Geoffrey Wheatcroft (*New York Times Book Review,* December 11, 2005), the region "is in the throes of a historically immense, pathological crisis whose character we only partly understand although we can perceive easily enough that what is already perilous may turn catastrophic, and could yet engulf us all." Others are equally loud in sounding the alarm bells. Thomas Friedman underscored the global threat by pointing out that "the world is drifting dangerously toward a widespread religious and sectarian cleavage the likes of which we have not seen for a long, long time." (*The New York Times*, February 24, 2006)

Mustafa Kemal's leadership helped Turkey navigate safely through dangerous waters and yet it took the young republic a couple of decades to cleanse the stains of past dependencies. Today, the conditions prevailing in the neighborhood demand an equally skillful leadership.

It is a sad commentary about the caliber of the present Turkish leadership to say that it will be the duty of future generations to break the shackles allowed by this cadre of mostly men who seem to have no vision other than reviving the symbols of Islam within the Turkish society.

4

A COALITION
OF THE CORRUPT

Of all the challenges facing the Turkish Republic, none is more insidious and threatening to the future of the regime than corruption. It has spread its tentacles within the business establishment, big and small; among the bureaucracy, including the judiciary, the security forces, and even the armed forces; and, among the elected members of the legislature and the governing elite.

The scope and the magnitude of the plundering, to which the nation's treasury and the Turkish taxpayers have been subjected, could only have been possible with the collusion of all three segments of society: the crooked businessmen needed the help of corrupt bureaucrats to legitimize their misdeeds, and the loopholes were made possible by helpful legislators. Powerful ministers and their cronies usually have their say when it comes to handing out millions, if not billions, of dollars' worth of contracts. And for the few who had the misfortune of being caught, there were the predictable amnesty laws custom made to save them.

When a former admiral of the Turkish navy was charged with misappropriation of state funds, public graft, receiving bribes and corruption in official capacity, it was clear that the rot had finally reached the heart of the patient. For, over the years, surveys have consistently indicated that, among all national institutions and professions, the Turkish Armed Forces was the one institution people trusted the most to be honest and reliable. When a high-ranking officer suffers such an indignity, the message is loud and clear.

The damage caused by the corrupt practices of the business community, has been the most severe. Since 1980, all controls over foreign capital movements were lifted and the internal marketplace was exposed to the merciless influence of short-term hot-money infusions.

During the Özal era, private-sector investments were mostly directed away from the productive and toward the speculative. In fact, the only policy considered worth pursuing was that of securing foreign capital, irrespective of the speculative nature of the incoming money, which was ready to pack up and leave on short notice. Simultaneously, the regime kept borrowing internally in order to meet its obligations. Sensing an opening, corrupt businessmen used and abused state banking laws and began financing the state treasury at astronomical interest rates using funds deposited at their banks. Such deposits were then systematically funneled to businessmen's other activities and acquisitions, as well as their offshore accounts. And when many of these banks declared their inability to meet their obligations, the state assumed their liabilities—to the tune of 50 to 80 billion dollars.

According to a report titled *The Economy of Waste*, prepared in 2001 by Faruk Türkoğlu for the Turkish Association of Chambers and Banks, the total financial loss suffered by the Turkish Treasury during the period 1990–2000 surpassed $195 billion. The report accused successive governments of sacrificing the growth potential of the national economy at the altar of short-term political gain. It identified the real culprit as the need for internal borrowing caused by undisciplined public-sector spending, which it called the "black hole" of the economy.

However, a regular student of the Turkish political and economic scene could immediately recognize the real "black hole" when in 2001, successive law-enforcement operations (code named "Operation White Energy," "Operation Hurricane," "Operation Parachute," "Operation Buffalo," "Operation Whale," "Operation Storm," "Operation Matador," "Operation Act No.1," "Operation Harvest," "Operation Fog," and "Operation Eagle") were launched against some of the major captains of the economy while other arms of the administration were busy shutting down the operations of several banks and assuming the administration of many others. Abuse of public trust, abuse of power, corruption, bribery, and embezzlement of public funds were the common themes among these various "operations." In each case, there was a symbiotic relationship between the businessman, the bureaucrat, the Mafioso, and the politician. In one case, improbable as it sounds, a businessman was able to purchase a bank for about $94 million by securing $93.5 million from the very same bank!

◆   ◆   ◆

Of course, the corruption of bankers was easily matched by the cunning of other businessmen who sought lucrative export subsidies by using bogus documents declaring fictitious export revenues, and by professionals who tried every trick in their arsenal in order not to pay taxes to the treasury. The collection of millions of euros by unscrupulous Islamic charities in Europe—in Germany, Holland, and Belgium in particular—is, in itself, a story of greed, ignorance and misplaced trust.

On October 18, 2005, Transparency International (TI) issued its "Corruption Perceptions Index (CPI) 2005." In its report, TI stated that "more than two-thirds of the 159 nations surveyed in TI's 2005 CPI scored less than 5 out of a clean score of 10, indicating serious levels of corruption." Turkey ranks sixty-fifth among the 159 nations, tied with Ghana, Mexico, Panama, and Peru. Turkey's CPI score is 3.5.

David Nussbaum, TI's chief executive, views corruption not a natural disaster but rather as a cold, calculated theft of opportunity from the men, women, and children who are least able to protect themselves. As for TI's Chairman Peter Eigen, corruption is a major cause of poverty as well as a barrier to overcoming it. He observed that the two scourges feed off each other, locking their populations in a cycle of misery.

Just as revealing as the corruption case of the admiral is a story divulged by none other than Bülent Arınç, the speaker of the Parliament. On the thirtieth anniversary of the founding of a hospital in Ankara, he lamented that his office had to deal with thousands of false and forged medical bills submitted by members of Parliament. "Why would one need to renew a prescription for reading glasses every two months?" he asked. He went on to admit that there were even those who had shamelessly submitted claims for tooth implants administered simultaneously to all of their thirty-two teeth!

Each year, the directorate of income tax publishes an average taxpayer profile for every professional discipline. The report published in 2005 for the income tax year 2004 reveals some hilarious if not ominous trends. It paints a picture of tax evasion among the well-to-do citizenry reaching obscene levels: In 2004 jewelers declared, on average, an annual taxable income of $320, while travel and tourism bureaus declared $220, furniture makers $200, furriers $170, and dental laboratories $115. Hotel owners who charge $115–150 per night for a single room declared an average annual taxable income of $370, while medical doctors who charge between $80 and $150 per patient were able to cut down their taxable income to just $700. According to their declarations, the taxable incomes of businessmen and professionals were not even close to those of primary school graduates employed by the state as doormen or janitors.

The percentage share of the income tax revenues to total tax revenues dropped from 52 percent in 1980 to 17 percent in 2005. As for corporate tax revenues, they too are gradually eroding, dropping from 10.3 percent of overall tax revenues in 2003 to 9.6 percent in 2004 and 7.5 percent in 2005. Since the indirect tax burden falls most heavily on the low-income citizen, it is clear that this government's policy is not to seek social justice and protect those least fortunate but rather to cater to those who will support the regime's corrupt practices.

The latest picture shows a religious party and its officers—at all levels and accross the country—mired in multiple scandals, some small and petty and others quite large and audacious. They are the latest practitioners of the unremitting corruption that has marked Turkish politics over the past half-century.

Part of the blame should go to the electorate, which has not elected good people into power. But a major portion of the blame should rests squarely on the shoulders of the political elite, who continue to treat the apparatus of the state as booty, selling influence for personal gain, taking kickbacks to award lucrative government contracts, and engaging in patronage, nepotism, bribery, pilfering of public funds, and funneling of state funds into private charity organizations. The net effect of such official graft is the decay of government institutions and the stunting of economic growth.

◆   ◆   ◆

The Justice and Development Party (AKP) have been in power since 2002. The list of corruption charges directed against this administration is quite long and substantial. It illustrates the scope of the decay within the body politics. Indeed, a list containing sixty different corruption allegations was detailed by a civil society group and circulated under the title *An Address to the Nation.* In its introduction, the report quotes a Turkish saying: "He who touches honey will lick his finger!" The most striking similarity among the various corruption allegations is the fact that, in most instances of public corruption, tenders have always been awarded either through no-bid contracts or to someone associated with the regime. The charges involving the Finance Minister Kemal Unakıtan are some of the most serious. Many of them involve tax evasion, fraud, forgery, and organized criminal activities. (See the Website kemalabi.com; also, Emel Armutçu, *Hürriyet,* February 5, 2006.)

Just as troubling are the close relationships between some party officials and Islamic holdings. The case of Kombassan Holding is a typical one. Founded by religious conservatives from Konya, it grew rapidly by issuing so-called shares in exchange for remittance income from Turkish workers living in Germany, Holland, France, and Belgium. The company funded the activities of various political movements, the most visible being the Refah Party of former Prime Minister

Necmettin Erbakan and his former partners Erdoğan and Gül. It is estimated that during the 1990s, Turkish workers in Europe remitted between $3 and $5 billion to Islamist holding companies. But when the authorities ordered Kombassan Holding to repay to the shareholders the millions of dollars they were entitled to, it became apparent that the shareholders had no leg to stand on. The company had not issued formal share certificates bearing the names of the individual owners.

This brings us to the case of Endüstri Holding, another Islamist company with similar practices. Its former director general, Ramazan Arıkan, created quite a furor when he asked his so-called shareholders to "drink a glass of water", a Turkish expression for a hopeless recovery. Mr. Arıkan, more recently, in an open letter to columnist Emin Çölaşan, divulged in great details the inner workings of a holding company (*Hürriyet,* September 1, 2005). In his words, these companies are nothing but glorified "pyramid schemes." They would tell people that it is a sin to save and not to spend for the glory of Allah and that the only way to spend for the glory of Allah would be to remit their funds to Islamic holding companies investing in good causes and providing returns of 25 to 40 percent! The operators of this scam used a TV station, which they established with the shareholders' remittances, to ask for more funds. From here, they broadcast pictures of non-existent factories and buildings in order to convince the faithful of the righteousness of their deeds. In Mr. Arıkan's opinion, the present regime will not do much to curb this pyramid scheme. He asserts that those who benefit from this game will never try to change the rules.

According to Sinan Aygün, president of the Ankara Chamber of Commerce, "swindlers with Islamist masks" and using religious references such as the theme of "profit without interest," have defrauded Turkish workers in Europe for an amount approaching 15 billion euros. It is, after the big banking scandals, the second-largest financial fraud recorded in the annals of the republic.

◆   ◆   ◆

History provides us with a few good examples of nations pulling themselves up by their bootstraps and, within a few generations, rising to standards of living unimaginable by their ancestors. Japan and Sweden come to mind. At the turn of the twentieth century, Sweden was a destitute country. Folkhemmet (People's Home) raised Sweden from its poor agrarian origins to an industrialized nation that provides generously for its people's human needs. What was the secret of their success? How did Sweden banish poverty and provide a decent standard of living for to its people?

While searching for the answer, I was struck by the caliber of the men who led Sweden during that period. Prime Minister Albin Hansson, in particular, epitomizes the character of the men who were governing the nation. Considered the father of the Folkhemmet, Hansson died in a manner typical of the way he always lived. Returning by streetcar from an official dinner in honor of the visiting Norwegian prime minister to his home in a poor suburb of Stockholm, he dropped dead as he stepped off the streetcar and was found by an astonished passerby, who recognized him at once.

Today, Turkey's political elite is so detached from its roots, so surrounded by bodyguards, that it would be unthinkable to witness a similar scenario. When Swedish Prime Minister Tage Erlander assumed the duties of his office, he had to take the oath of office in the presence of King Gustav V. Erlander hesitated to place two fingers on the Bible in the traditional manner, saying that he did not believe much in God. The king's reply was just as emblematic of the tolerant political climate of the country: "I don't see why you should worry—perhaps He doesn't believe too much in you, either." In contrast, the religious fervor of present-day Turkish leaders is almost unbelievable.

Sweden's spectacular rise was not due to "privatization" or "accession to a European Union" or even "globalization." It was the result of sheer hard work, dedication, honest government, and sensible social programs aimed at achieving social justice. Indeed, the Social Democratic Party's platform stated that the party's chief objective was "maintaining full employment no matter what happened." It underlined the importance of this policy by declaring that "no able-bodied man or woman should suffer enforced idleness any longer than is necessary." It also called upon the government to encourage the export industries, promote agricultural loans and subsidies, carry out extensive housing programs, undertake public works, combat business monopolies by entering into competition through cooperatives, implement the state takeover of any industry that became too powerful, and nationalize the coal industry and the importation of oil.

The party platform set several goals remarkable for their ambitious nature:

- Higher pay for farmers in order to bring their income up to the level of industrial workers

- Unemployment insurance to cover all work

- Shorter working hours, longer vacations

- Compulsory universal health insurance covering hospital and medical care and maternity benefits
- Higher pensions for old age, the invalid, and the blind
- Better facilities for higher education
- Compulsory schooling for nine to ten years instead of seven to eight years
- Equal pay for similar work
- Leveling of wealth through taxation
- Limits on large private estates

Many of these goals were achieved in the 1950s. In fact, the parliament that followed the 1952 elections was referred to as the "Parliament of Great Reforms." In retrospect, these reforms were achieved by men and women whose loyalty were to the welfare of their nation as a whole and who did not hesitate to go against all powerful business interests. By comparison, Turkey's political elite are a bunch of hired men consumed by their desire to enrich themselves and servile to their patrons, the party bosses.

Recently, a gentle nudge came from none other than the man responsible for Turkish affairs at the economic desk of the European Union Commission. Dirk Verbeken, whose job it is to monitor the economic trends in Turkey, admitted that there is a group within the government that is accorded special treatment during privatization activities. The comments were offered in response to media reports describing a number of suspicious transactions:

- leasing of the most valuable asset (Galataport) along the Bosphorus, to a friend of the regime
- modification by the Parliament, during a late night session, of the law governing the shorelines in order to benefit the same benefactor
- adoption of an amnesty law, custom made to regularize the status of buildings illegally erected at another port city
- secret sale, in contravention to previously adopted procedures and to the same individual, of 15 percent of the shares of the Turkish Refinery TÜPRAŞ, the value of which increased significantly over the next two weeks, thus enriching the buyer by several hundred millions of dollars. Even more puzzling was that a meeting between the businessman and the prime minister took place in a hotel suite just the night before the sale.

◆   ◆   ◆

More recently, Prime Minister Erdoğan shifted his travel itineraries from the West to the Arab world. In a highly publicized exchange of visits, he and Dubai's heir to the throne, Prince Sheik Muhammad Bin Rashid Al Maktum, came to an understanding regarding real estate investments Dubai is considering for Istanbul—totaling about $5 billion. During a visit to Jeddah, Saudi Arabia, the Prime Minister is said to have offered to Prince Velid bin Talal bin Abdulaziz a choice Bosphorus location for a new Savoy Hotel to be added to his hotel chain.

All of these negotiations, discussions, and offers have one thing in common. They were not open to public bidding.

The problem, to put it bluntly, is the absence of transparency. Establishing a procedure whereby politicians' and public servants' income is made public would go a long way towards restoring public confidence.

At a seminar in Zagreb, Croatia, organized jointly by the Guardian Forum and the British Association, topics including corruption, organized crime, terror, and the media's approach to these issues was discussed. It was observed that in Turkey and in many southeastern European countries, it is vital to question sources of wealth, especially the sudden accumulation of wealth, in order to resolve issues such as corruption and organized crime. Explications such as "gift" or "thanks to my relatives" are common. Moreover, the required secrecy of these declarations regarding the office holder's worth is a serious impediment to keeping corruption in check. Compare the current British practice of making statements accessible through the Internet with the Turkish practice, which keeps statements submitted by politicians secret. As a consequence of this policy of opaqueness, it was possible for the Turkish Prime Minister to continue to be the distributor of Ülker biscuits. When the media reported that he had sold his share in the company, they focused more on the amount of money he collected than what else he was looking to sell. In fact, it was known for some time that he owned a soft drink distributorship as well.

The minister of state in charge of finance, and now chief negotiator for the accession talks with the EU, Ali Babacan, also has a serious conflict-of-interest problem. He owns shares in a family business, and he has shown no intention to transfer them or to place them in a blind trust.

Needless to say, until an independent institution verifies that the incomes of political figures are in line with their lifestyles and expenditures, we can't expect to see any significant inroads in the fight against corruption.

On another front, there was a hopeful development, courtesy of the Turkish Armed Forces' Military Tribunal. In the case of the admiral mentioned earlier, the court found him guilty of corruption. In addition to a jail sentence, it ordered the repossession of his two luxury villas on the grounds that the admiral could not have acquired them on his income. Furthermore, the court did not buy the defense's argument that generous friends and relatives had assisted him in the purchase. It declared, "Such a generous act, well beyond the means of the relatives, would fly in the face of the realities of life!" Now, let us hope that all politicians will soon be asked the same question: "When and how did you get it?"

◆   ◆   ◆

The business pages of the Turkish dailies are replete with news about the sales of big properties, major companies, and top money-making corporations. The most remarkable thing about these sales is not that they're taking place but rather that the buyers usually have no known histories and mysterious sources of income. In short, the economy is passing from the hands of "old money" to those whose fortune is of "unknown origin." These people all seem to have a common background: They were dirt poor, doing all sorts of menial jobs. Then, in the past few years, they worked their butts off and became rich. In response to such tall tales, Güngör Uraş, a columnist for the national daily *Milliyet*, reminds us of a Turkish saying: "You either never experienced a beating, or you don't know how to count." Uraş maintains that the amounts involved in these transactions are not the kind one could save "by selling pistachios or filberts."

According to Uraş, even more troublesome is that these transactions are done out in the open. The amounts paid are known to all parties. So, he wonders, how is it possible that people who do not appear on anyone's taxpayer lists are suddenly capable of acquiring companies or real estates for up to $600 million, and why are state tax agencies reluctant to check their books? That the Turkish economy is rapidly changing hands and the new captains of this economy may turn out to be of rather questionable character is a rather disturbing development.

There is a popular Turkish saying: "When a fish begins to rot, its head stinks first!" ("*Balık baştan kokar!*") This aptly summarizes the current state of the Turkish political landscape. Indeed, stories about tax evasion, fictitious exports, sham invoices, money laundering, embezzlement, and the misappropriation of state funds appear regularly in the national dailies. What is most frustrating is that many of the people engaged in these illegal activities are all presently protected from prosecution behind a shield of "immunity."

During the 2002 election campaign, the AKP promised to change the immunity law and limit its scope to a Member of Parliament's speeches and debates. But unfortunately, the party's parliamentary majority relied on the votes of deputies who were facing serious corruption charges. Thus, the likelihood of an amendment to the present law was nil. It has been more than three years since those election promises were made. Nothing has changed and nothing will.

For others, including the Prime Minister, there was another more pressing challenge. The PM owned several distributorships, and these companies were facing tax evasion charges. Therefore, immediately following their assumption of power, AKP began to draft a new bill dealing with "tax amnesty," and on February 27, 2003, the "Tax Reconciliation Law" was enacted. Its declared goal was to achieve "social peace." But in reality, the law was an ingenious device whereby the responsible authorities were barred from reviewing the income tax declaration of a taxpayer who was willing to submit an amended declaration in which tax liabilities were increased. The minimum taxable income amendment was set at about $8,000. The two companies partly owned by the prime minister did not waste a minute and amended their previous declarations. It enabled both companies to close their tax books for past years to any future inspection even though, for the year 2000, one of the companies had declared, previously, no texable income.

◆   ◆   ◆

Recep Tayyip Erdoğan's troubles with the law can be traced all the way to the days when, as mayor of Greater Istanbul, he was involved in a slew of activities deemed questionable by prosecutors. In early 2002, both Recep Tayyip Erdoğan, who served as mayor from 1994 to 1998, and his successor, Ali Müfit Gürtuna, who took over in 1998, faced multiple charges, including embezzlement, misappropriation of state funds, public graft, abuse of power, fraud in the execution of tenders, and participation in organized criminal activities.

But Turkey was heading towards a general election, and the front-runner was the AKP. All efforts were thus directed towards delaying the outcome of the court proceedings until the November 3, 2002, elections. On the morning of November 4, Turks woke up and realized that a new regime, and a new ruling class, was about to take over. From that day on, the fate of Erdoğan was no longer in the hands of the judiciary. Indeed, within a brief few months, the charges brought against the whole gang of municipal chiefs, directors, and the mayor were suddenly found to be baseless. It was as if the charges of corruption brought against the mayor—the leasing of the municipality's TV station to a company controlled by the Nakşibendi Brotherhood (Iskenderpaşa Convent) and the vast amount of advertising revenues channeled to a new TV channel (Kanal 7); the leasing of municipality-owned billboards (1250 of them) to a company controlled by the same Nakşibendi Order for a pittance; the tales of corruption in the awarding of contracts by the municipality-owned natural gas distribution company (IGDAŞ); the celebrated "virtual embezzlement" case involving the electronic ticket sale and distribution by the municipality-owned company (AKBIL); the unending saga of the "ALBAYRAKLAR" and their lucrative construction, service, and trash collection contracts, some dealing with the construction of the Istanbul subway; and some ten or more other reported cases of corruption—were just figments of a prosecutor's imagination. Were they?

Here is what Harun Karaca, a municipal employee, said during his deposition:

> Recep Tayyip Erdoğan empowered me to negotiate with the companies we awarded contracts to regarding the percentage of commission they were expected to pay. I submitted to the mayor all dossiers issued by the office of the general secretary. Therefore, I was the first one to meet with those deemed eligible to bid and also with the award winner. We would meet to decide whom we would award the contract to. The mayor had to approve of the company, and the company had to have views agreeable with ours. I would meet with the owner of the winning bid in my office on the floor where the mayor's office is located, and later I would arrange for him to meet with Ahmet Ergün. He would collect the money.

The saga of Albayraklar-Erdoğan connection is ongoing. The government's privatization arm, the State Board for Privatization, recently sold the SEKA Paper Plant to the Group Albayraklar, along with its hundreds of acres of land, shops, machinery, and housing, for a mere $1.1 million. What's more, the government ignored a court order vacating the sale. It took the Superior Court for Administration (Danıştay) to finally order the administration to initiate a judicial inquiry against those who caused the treasury to suffer such heavy losses. No one expects the government to respect the court's directive. After all, this regime may talk the talk but will not walk the walk, may say that it respects the rule of law, but its actions indicate otherwise.

Currently, eighty-three MPs of the AKP are hiding behind a shield of "parliamentary immunity." The dossiers of twenty-one of these involve cases of corruption, including charges brought against the Prime Minister and four of his top cabinet ministers: Minister of Foreign Affairs Abdullah Gül, Interior Minister

Abdülkadir Aksu, Finance Minister Kemal Unakıtan, and Agriculture Minister Mehdi Eker.

More recently, the PM and his party got a jolt: a revolt of their intellectual base. The fact that old allies of the regime had to raise their voice illustrates the corrosive effect of corruption on the morale of the party faithful. The voice heard in the Internet Web site "Knowledge and Divine Wisdom" (*www.bilgihik-met.com*) was a familiar one for the readers of pro-government daily *Zaman*. Indeed Ali Bulaç has, until now, been an ardent supporter of the PM. But it seems he has now had his fill of the corruption that has spread throughout the economy. In his first salvo (*Bilgi ve Hikmet,* January 22, 2006), he framed the debate very clearly:

> The question which we need to answer is: Should this have been the end point of a struggle dating back almost two hundred years? Can those who do not sweat, suffer, or pay any price be allowed to steal and convert to their benefit the sweat, the suffering, and the price paid by others? And if they do, then what happens?

A few days later, Ali Bulaç clearly illustrated the charges against this regime: "We have not discarded an ideology after exploiting it; we did not sever our old ties with the past as soon as we reached the pinnacle; we did not pocket the money of the poor and act as if nothing had happened." The ultimate insult was yet to come:

> Are the unethical behavior and the irresponsible lifestyles of those in leadership positions and the ideology of this political movement reconcilable? Is this what we call "conservative democracy?" It is obvious that the house is filled with dirt. You will not be able to remove it by simply shoving it under the furniture and the rugs.

Coming from an ideologue of political Islam, these are fiery words, and those of us who also believe that the house is filling with dirt should welcome these words of reason. Ali Bulaç went a bit further in a recent article (*Bilgi ve Hikmet,* February 11, 2006), in which he ventured to predict the future:

> To misrepresent for the sake of power is immoral...At present, a small clique—a few years ago they were ardent Islamists—are sitting at the head of the spring, holding all power centers, and as they fill their pockets, they belittle and degrade Muslims...Those who today shave their beard and even go to bed with their neckties, tomorrow will not be seen around. They are passen-

gers; we are the innkeepers. Tomorrow, they will hide in their million-dollar homes hidden in the midst of a forest and will zip through our neighborhood in their "Hummer" jeeps...

The AKP faithful who are sitting at the head of the spring may not agree with the basic philosophy of such an Islamist intellectual, but they better pay attention to the message.

◆　　◆　　◆

There is another saying in Turkish that is perhaps even more appropriate to the present circumstances: "When the *imam* farts, the congregation shits." So, were the leaders of this administration good role models? In fact, what was the rest of the population doing?

For one thing, Ömer Dinçer, undersecretary for the prime ministry, has been found guilty of plagiarism (October 21, 2005). On two occasions, he and his co-author, Yahya Fidan copied sentences, paragraphs, even full pages—including all the misspellings—verbatim from the works of others. Even though the charge of plagiarizing the work of Prof. Dr. Tamer Koçel, in their book titled *Business Administration*, was dropped due to the statute of limitations, they were not so lucky with their 2003 book, *Introduction to Business Administration*. Had the commission charged with evaluating the book waited one more month, the charges of plagiarism would have again been subject to the statute of limitations rule, and the undersecretary for the prime ministry would have gotten off. Instead, he was found to be a cheat by a vote of fourteen to five—with all five not-guilty votes cast by commission members appointed by the government.

But Prof. Dinçer was not the poster child of a corrupt ruling class. There are others who could lay claim to such a title. On September 18, 2005, during the television program *Arena* on CNN-Türk, director Uğur Dündar divulged to the public secret details of the attempted escape of Mr. and Mrs. Yahya Murat Demirel. Demirel is the man responsible of bankrupting Egebank by misappro-priating over $1 billion of the bank's money. He is also the nephew of Süleyman Demirel, a former president of the republic. On New Year's Eve, he and his wife were apprehended by the Bulgarian coast guard as they were attempting to leave Turkey, even though there was a hold on his passport. It is now reported in the media that Y. M. Demirel had several secret bank accounts in a Merrill Lynch branch office in the Cayman Islands and he established several companies on the Isle of Man and in Singapore. In fact, the name of one of the companies (Barla

Finance Limited) appears to have been inspired by the village of Barla, in the Province of Isparta, where several members of the Demirel clan own summer cottages.

A survey carried out among the top one hundred taxpayers of the country provides another example of the decadent nature of Turkish business ethics. It revealed that the names of some of the wealthiest families are not even listed. Yet the public knows that the fortunes of some of them are far greater than the fortunes of those appearing on the list. It appears that some of the wealthiest men in Turkey did not have any tax liabilities in 2004.

◆   ◆   ◆

Rampant corruption, at all levels of a society, cannot be checked and eradicated without removing the very shield under which sleaze flourishes in the first place. In this respect, the main culprit is the immunity enjoyed by elected parliamentarians and high level bureaucrats. It is a cardinal rule of political science that power attracts sleaze balls. As long as the atmosphere they operate in is conducive to the flourishing of sleaze, it is nearly impossible to eradicate corruption. What is needed, therefore, is transparency.

The governing party, AKP, prior to the 2002 elections, promised quite a few logical reforms. However, "that was then and this is now," in the words of former president Demirel who used the expression when he was Prime Minister to explain the ease with which he could take diametrically opposite positions on certain issues. Under article 2.2, titled "Political Principles," AKP's election platform promised "to have politics and politicians back in a respectable and confidence inspiring position." And further stated that: "The most basic need of the political institutions in our country is for politics to have a structure where honesty and integrity are basic, where political financing can be accountable and transparent." (AKParti.org.tr, English Web site)

However, the party program's stated goals are far removed from today's realities. The latest survey by Transparency International, a global coalition against corruption, published under the title *Global Corruption Barometer 2005*, reveals that in the past three years, corruption in Turkey has increased significantly. Furthermore, in a survey commissioned by the AKP itself, nearly 60 percent of the respondents qualified as a failure the regime's attempts to curb corruption. Worse yet, the respondents consider the political parties to be among the most corrupt institutions, along with tax and customs officials, the police, the judiciary, the private business sector, and Parliament. As in past surveys, the military continues to retain the nation's highest level of trust and confidence.

The low level of trust expressed towards elected Members of Parliament stems from a near impossibility to prosecute a politician involved in corrupt practices while he is armed with the shield of "parliamentary immunity." Parliamentary immunity, which is supposed to protect MPs from prosecution for their acts and words as parliamentarians—similar to the speech and debate clause of the US Constitution-, has become a blanket with which all sorts of misdeeds are kept from the scrutiny of the law. And yet, on this issue too, AKP's 2002 electoral platform stated,

- Legislation shall be offered to prevent the pollution of politics.

- Politics shall end to be a vehicle for profiteering.

- All elected officials' declaration of personal fortune shall be made available for public information and scrutiny in a transparent manner. (AKParti.org.tr, English Web site)

Finally, the platform committed to take all necessary actions to remove the obstacles to prosecuting public officials. It promised to limit parliamentary immunity to acts carried out by a deputy in the performance of his or her duties as an elected member of the national assembly. (Immunity for speech and debate)

None of these promises were kept. And the party is buried, up to its neck, in a swamp of corruption, unable to move forward without alienating many of its members. Corporate hacks, fat cats, and sleaze balls thrive in such an environment. As for the leaders, they have become intellectually flabby, unable to inspire let alone lead. Their only remaining tactic is an old one: play the religious card.

But unfortunately, this tried and true gimmick suggests that this administration, and the country as a whole, has fallen victim to the ravages of crony capitalism. Various oligarchic clans have gained access to one or more seats of power within the administration. Unless they are tamed, the erosion of the foundations of the Kemalist republic will continue unabated.

Today, a conspicuous social divide separates a large segment of the populace, which is denied the basic necessities of life, from tiny elite that enjoys the best of life. As a result, the disintegration of the social fabric is noticeable everywhere. Suicides, bankruptcies, broken homes, street children, and highly educated youth seeking manual jobs are just a few signs of this cultural and social degradation.

The increasingly oligarchic nature of Turkish society and the inequalities it displays are the root cause of the rampant corruption sweeping the land. History tells us that highly unequal societies are highly corrupt, and such grievous inequalities among the citizenry are a major threat to the democratic character of a society.

Today, ministers charged with corruption and a PM who protects those accused of corruption are all hiding behind a shield of immunity and continue to turn a deaf ear. Ordinarily, the best remedy to such a corrupt system would be the development of a civil society keenly aware of the shortcomings of the state. In the case of Turkey, many of the groups that are part of the civil society were nurtured by donor support from the European Union (remember Karen Fogg?), the United States (PKK is still operating from northern Irak!), and private philanthropists like George Soros (was he not responsible for the economic collapse in Ukraine, and Georgia and Indonesia too?). Indeed, the EU commissars and Soros's Quantum Fund and the Open Society Institute were not too critical when the beneficiaries of Turkey's GDP growth were the same oligarchs. As for the government and its super majority in Parliament, they were not about to lift a finger to level the playing field. In short, from a latticework of corruption by big and small bureaucrats to shakedowns by officials connected to the corporate world to no-bid tenders by members of major ruling classes, the establishment always had the last word.

Having tamed the privately owned media, it appears the administration has put the question of diversifying ownership and ending the dominance of the oligarchies on the back burner. Transparency and the search for the truth via the media can wait a little longer!

◆   ◆   ◆

To be fair, corrupt practices are not limited to members of the national assembly. Equally grave are the telltale signs that the judiciary is not immune from such a threat. As high civil servants, the immunity they enjoy is just as frustrating as that of the parliamentarians. On October 8, 2004, the Disciplinary Council of the Supreme Court voted to remove one of its members from his seat on the bench and to "warn" another. They were implicated during the investigations carried out as part of Operation Lancet-2 (*Neşter-2*) and charged with abuse of public trust, conflict of interest, public graft, and attempt to influence the outcome of pending court cases, some of which concerned some of the country's most notorious Mafia figures.

The most glaring sign of the incestuous relationship between organized crime figures and the judiciary appeared recently in the media. "Let's get you a prosecutor at least!" says one gang leader to another, according to the transcripts of recorded telephone conversations. (*Milliyet*, February 27, 2006) The two participants were monitored by court order as part of an operation code named "Tulip." When the prosecution of a criminal case can be influenced by underground gangs operating with impunity, then the balances of justice are no longer serving the nation but rather the high and the mighty. The case calls to mind Alain Minc, a French intellectual who observed, some ten years ago, that the Mafiosi were the most significant economic class to emerge during the post-communist era. (*Le Nouveau Moyen Age*, Alain Minc, 1995) The Turkish crime syndicate, on the other hand, was and still is a subclass of the robber barons of the Turkish business, entertainment, and political elite.

Looking ahead to the next general election the picture remains cloudy. Presently, only the Republican People's Party (CHP) is represented in Parliament (TBMM-Grand National Assembly). However, the number of parties jockeying for a seat in the next Parliament is probably close to twenty. Many, if not most, suffer from a certain lack of vision, lack of purpose, and a lack of coherent message. Most, if not all, are herded by leaders who can make or break a political career by deciding who is placed on the ballot and in what order. The best example of "one-man rule" within a party was on display when the Party of the Democratic Left (DSP) of former Prime Minister Bülent Ecevit won big in 1999 and then literally disappeared from the scene after being clobbered during the 2002 elections. He and his wife, Rahşan Ecevit, were the absolute rulers within a party that tolerated no criticism.

Turkish electoral system is geared to accommodate those who are "in," leaving those on the outside frustrated and angry. All of this is not to suggest that the political establishment does not enjoy the participation of truly gifted scholars, bureaucrats, statesmen, jurists, writers, and others who are no doubt aware of the system's shortcomings. But the system is dysfunctional. And why were all these well trained and educated politicians willing to surrender their judgment and their independence to the whim of an autocratic ruler is beyond comprehension?

Today, it is very fashionable to demand that the state be reduced and rendered more or less impotent. The word 'devolution' has become quite popular. The push is coming from the supporters of the EU, from those who would like to move the present system towards a federation formed by its Kurdish and Turkish components and from the advocates of the second Republic, under which the Sharia would eventually emerge. They blame the state for all sorts of criminalities. The usual pejorative term used in this context has been to accuse the "deep state"from being responsible for actions of criminal elements operating underground.

What these advocates of an eviscerated Turkish state fail to grasp is that there can be no human rights, no rule of law, and no democracy without the state. The alternative, as witnessed during the final years of the Ottoman era, is anarchy and a state of insecurity. The friends of democracy and justice must strive to save the state from the irresponsible actions of those who may not have the best interests of the nation in mind.

Michael Rubin, editor of the *Middle East Quarterly*, in a hard-hitting article, summed it up best by contrasting what, a decade ago, was viewed as the influence of a "deep state"—a shadowy network of generals, intelligence officials and organized crime bosses-with present day's main topic, namely the influence of "green money" and the financial opacity of the AKP. Indeed, Rubin predicts that the Saudi money will eventually erode Turkish secularism.

> If the AKP is able to translate money into power and power into money, then the main loser will be Turkish secularism. As an executive with one of Istanbul's largest firms said, "AKP is like cancer. You feel fine, but then one day you start coughing blood. By the time you realize there's a problem, it's too far gone." (Michael Rubin, "Green Money, Islamist Politics in Turkey," *Middle East Quarterly*, winter 2005).

Recently, columnist Cüneyt Ülsever (*Hürriyet*, May 25, 2006), while urging the Prime Minister to call, for the sake of the regime, for snap elections, asked him a loaded question: "How well informed are you about the nature of the dossiers that are being prepared against you?"

The recent history of Turkish politics and politicians has been inextricably linked through such dossiers and files…Turkey certainly deserves a beter future than what this crew is offering.

◆   ◆   ◆

Corruption has many faces. One of the most insidious is called "patronage." The Islamist regime's efforts to systematically place their cronies in all sorts of positions or reward them with government contracts lead to many scandals. The following stories are some of the most egregious examples.

Children of an orphanage located in the city of Malatya became, overnight, the biggest topic among the national media. Thanks to a reporter's hidden camera, the daily savage beatings of these children became a major Prime-Time item.

After the exposure the attention quickly shifted from the gruesome details to those responsible for it. We learned through the media that the government had earlier submitted for the president's approval the name of one of their cronies as director general of the Organization for Social Services and Child Protection. But the president of the republic had turned the request down. As they had done on numerous other occasions, the regime then circumvented the approval process by making a temporary appointment. As a result, a man who had no prior experience in social services, or familiarity with a child protection organization, was now heading a vast network of orphanages and social service agencies as its "acting" director general. He packed the place with his cronies, especially those of similar ideology. Experienced personnel were replaced, and many were simply let go. The party hacks had achieved their desired patronage goal.

Next, it was the turn of the regional offices. Every one of these local orphanages received an appointee with close ties to the Administration. They, too, replaced current employees with totally unqualified personnel loyal to the party bosses. The man put in charge of the orphanage in Malatya had hired some women far less qualified than the trained teachers and supervisors they replaced. The new hires knew only one way to discipline children: by beating them.

The events in Malatya put the government on the defensive. They severely tested the conscience of the nation. And soon other dirty little secrets suddenly found their way to the front pages of the daily papers. A public already numbed by stories about family violence, honor killings, and child abuse were now seeing the ugly side of the so-called entrepreneurial spirit of some Turkish businessmen.

On the evening of October 30, 2005, two cable-TV channels, CNN-Türk and KanalD, presented a heartrending story of child labor in the brick factories of Tekirdağ, a province of Turkey on the European continent. Earlier that day, the TV crew received a tip detailing the distressing circumstances under which children (boys and even girls) were employed. A nine-year-old boy described the harsh working conditions: extreme dust, heavy lifting, ten-hour shifts, very modest diet, and living quarters infected with bed bugs. He was still waiting to get his first paycheck, based on a daily pay of about $7.

A pair of stories from the southern province of Hatay and the central Anatolian province of Amasya best illustrates the corruption by elected public servants and their bureaucrat cronies. Media reports, later confirmed by other elected officials, indicated that a vice-chairman of the AKP Parliamentary Group was directing local public officials in Hatay in the awarding of a host of public work projects to his cronies. As a result, the chairman, members of the party's provincial governing board, a member of the local disciplinary board, and the secretary of the local party branch were all awarded contracts for a variety of public work projects. It was also reported that several of these party hacks had not established businesses until well after the party won the 2002 elections (*Hürriyet*, February 11, 2006). In the province of Amasya, the mayor of the AKP-dominated Çorum municipality was accused of similar corrupt practices. How party cronies were rewarded was detailed on unsigned flyers placed in citizens' mailboxes.

◆   ◆   ◆

During the first three years of the Islamist regime, the damage inflicted on the economy, through corruption and mismanagement, was highlighted in a report issued (November 2005) by the Ankara Chamber of Commerce. In it the "state of the nation" was presented in gloomy terms:

- External debt has risen from $130.2 billion (in 2002) to $161.8 billion (by mid-June 2005).

- Internal debt has risen from $91.7 billion to $177 billion.

- Total debt (internal and external) registered an increase of $116.9 billion.

- Per-capita national debt increased by 45 percent in three years.

- The foreign trade deficit which in 2001 was recorded at $10 billion, increased by 54 percent in 2002, by another 43 percent in 2003, and by a whopping 56 percent in 2004, to reach an all-time record of $34.4 billion. The situation further deteriorated in 2005, when it reached $42.9 billion, an increase of 25 percent over 2004.

- The account deficit has ballooned from $1.56 billion (2002) to $8 billion (2003) to $15.5 billion (2004) to $22.8 billion (as of December 31, 2005). In short, the current account deficit has increased tenfold in just three years and now represents 6.4 percent of the gross national product.

- Hot money entering the country has artificially raised the value of the local currency, thus aggravating the already shaky trade deficit by distorting the cost differential between imported goods and locally manufactured ones. It has made Turkish exports less competitive in world markets. When growth rates are predicated on increased importation rather than increased production of goods, such growth is always short lived.

- The number of taxpayers has decreased from 1.77 million to 1.70 million in three years. The inevitable consequence of this deterioration has been the increase in the ratio of indirect to direct tax revenues. It is now at an all-time high of 70 percent.

- Under the forced diet administered by the International Monetary Fund, the government devotes 6.5 percent of the budget (after interest payments) to debt payments. Consequently, the amount of funds directed towards productive investments has shrunk from 2.4 percent of the gross national product in 2001 to just 1.8 percent in 2004. Under such draconian measures, there is no chance of combating poverty, youth unemployment, and a widening income gap.

As a local Midwestern farmer would say: "Figures don't lie...but liers figure."

It was none other than Vice-Premier Abdüllatif Şener who, recently, provided the most telling figure about the social consequences of the government's economic mismanagement: "18 million citizens are living below the powerty limit." (May 26, 2006)

◆   ◆   ◆

Thus, within three short years, a popularly elected government proved to be totally incompetent. By repeating the mistakes of old regimes, they have failed to reverse the course of corruption, as they promised they would. Ethics, morals, honesty, and transparency have become hollow words in the mouth of these politicians.

The criminal behavior of political cronies who will not admit that their first duty is to protect the welfare of the children placed under their care; the inhumane treatment of children by adults whose sole objective is to enrich themselves; the nepotism by party bosses who will favor party loyalty over competence, are all variations on the same theme: crimes that make a mockery of the "social justice" clause of the constitution. And now, to add insult to injury, we are told that Turks with deep pockets have already bought up all the units of Ferrari's newest model, the "Fiorano," allocated to Turkey—well before its selling price has been announced. For those who earn this kind of dirty money in a land where one out of every four lives below the threshold of poverty, these are signs of an ugly "Dolce Vita."

Following recent arrests in Antalya, the authorities uncovered a criminal gang, the members of which included three police officers, one prison guard, and a court official. That officers of the law who have sworn to uphold the law and protect the citizenry were found to be engaged in criminal activities may not be earthshaking. But when it becomes just a small piece of the larger picture one has to pay attention. Even more serious evidence came to light when the media uncovered the story of officials who provided physical disability reports to the sons of the rich, for as much as $20 to $40 thousand, thus enabling them to evade the military draft. Meanwhile, in the administrative districts of Şemdinli and Yüksekova of the eastern Province of Hakkari, near the borders with Iran and Iraq, local security forces appear to have taken the law into their own hands, while some local merchants were willingly cooperating with the PKK, and with the ever-present drug lords.

Turkish political landscape is dominated today by a "culture of corruption". It has become a way of life. What is in short supply is a sense of righteousness, of national rectitude and compassion, and values like honesty, decency, and fairness.

Today, thanks to corporate corruption no one is sure anymore whose hand is in whose pocket. There is only one absolute reality: through their local mercenaries, the hands of the multinationals and corporate moguls are in every citizen's pocket. In such a climate, where truth and honesty are already on life-support, whether government leaders are out to insult the intelligence of the average citizen or are merely fools is a distinction without a difference.

The question of what to say to future generations is a difficult one. In the words of Kurt Vonnegut "psychopathic personalities, which is to say persons without conscience, without senses of pity or shame have taken all the money." (Kurt Vonnegut, *A Man without a Country*, 2005) The description quite accurately applies to members of the Turkish ruling oligarchy.

5

A MEDIA OF MOGULS

Saturday, October 29, 2005, late night...

My Internet connection to everything Turkish begins, every night, with the reading of the following day's Turkish dailies, starting with the columnists for the *Hürriyet*. Given Turkey's mounting problems and the compelling need for intellectual discourse, I was a bit surprised to discover that Ertuğrul Özkök, managing editor of the influential Istanbul daily *Hürriyet*, would choose to entertain his readers with a pompous and fluffy article. Granted, among columnists, there seems to be an unwritten rule that Sundays are for showing one's literary talent. I have never figured out why, but I suspect, for some, "Never on Sunday" rule means "no politics on holidays."

> It was morning, 7:00 A.M. The mountains around Lake Como were high and the sun had not yet risen. As for the crescent moon, it was refusing to set. Bach's 3rd suite in C-major was playing. The smell of fresh coffee was spinning my head. It was one of those moments when one is afraid of dying. And yet all of Italy was getting ready to celebrate All-Saints Day. At precisely that very moment, I was reading a strange love story. In the Hotel Villa d'Este, that jewel of Lake Como, in a room overlooking the lake, I was trying to understand a woman's fear of losing her lover.

My first reaction was that of someone who senses his interlocutor's irresistible temptation for "name dropping." The writer was giving us a charming prince (Ottavio Gallilos), an architect (Pellegrino Pellegrini), a nobleman, a young ballerina, and many more. I tried to imagine myself in a little teahouse in the Anatolian hinterland where an average Mehmet has his morning tea while connecting with the gentleman at the other end of this narrative. I could almost hear him: "What are you talking about?"

For me the disconnect was due to a totally different reason. Having been conditioned, daily, with a stiff dose of *NYT* columnists, it was impossible to imagine former and present columnists, Safire, Kristoff, Friedman, or Brooks devoting a full column to such fluff. They would connect with their readers with letters from Darfur and Bangalore, from Tibet or Shanghai. But in a world facing hunger, powerty and social upheavals, in a country whose future is on the line, do a responsible media have the luxury to engage their readers with such peripheral issues? I doubt it very much. Yet in Turkey, intellectuals have a burning desire to show off their stuff. So, on another Sunday, November 6, 2005, I am happy to report that Özkök's head was spinning again, but this time with "The Pearl Fishers" of Bizet.

◆   ◆   ◆

I wanted to begin the issue of the responsibilities of the Turkish media with a gentle ribbing. Of course, the Turkish media's problems are a lot more serious than a few columnists taking their Sunday strolls in the playgrounds of the rich and famous. And the problems are sui-generis.

In Turkey, the press is controlled by media barons who wish to use the influence of their papers to extend the reach of their far-flung business "empires." There are four major dailies with circulations of 400,000 or more. Eleven others have circulations in excess of 100,000. Overall, daily newspaper circulation is about five million, and almost half of that total is controlled by the Doğan Group (*Posta, Hürriyet, Milliyet, Vatan, Fanatik, Radikal,* and the *Turkish Daily News*). The circulation of another major group of papers (*Sabah, Takvim, and Fotomaç*) is almost a million. The religious and right-wing media controls the rest. The lone voice of the Kemalist left, *Cumhuriyet,* commands no more than 60,000 (*gazeteciler.com,* October 6, 2005).

Ever since the 2001 Turkish financial crisis, the Turkish media has experienced a fundamental transformation. No longer can one speak of independent journalism and independent newspapers. Capitalists with deep pockets have acquired several journals and TV/radio stations and engaged in a merciless battle to dominate the sector. Moreover, these media barons, who have other businesses unrelated to their publishing activities, have used their access to the media as a weapon against their competitors or the government. And when it is a question of winning a government contract the idea of independent journalism was easily forgotten in favor of manipulating the news for selfish interest. The use of reporters and columnists as "hit men" became a fact of life.

During the past decade, several large industrial and financial groups chose to "arm" themselves by acquiring a TV station or a newspaper for the purpose of intimidation. The collision between media giants was no more than a reflection of their desire to dominate other sectors of the economy. If the free press is the oxygen of a free society, then it might be appropriate to refer to Turkey as asthmatic.

Today, several media groups are owned by businessmen whose banks and business empires have failed spectacularly and had to rely on the generosity and forgiveness of the government regulators to survive. There is the Uzan Family group (petrochemicals, electric power utilities, Star TV, daily *Star*, Imar Bank, and Ada Bank). They swindled The Motorola and Nokia group out of a couple of billion dollars. Later they defrauded their own banks out of almost $20 billion. Another big-time operator, Mehmet Emin Karamehmet (Daily *Akşam*, Show TV, Pamukbank, and Yapı Kredi Bankası) was accused of financing his other business ventures through fraudulent transactions totaling $6.2 billion using one of his banks, Pamukbank. There was a third character, Dinç Bilgin (daily *Sabah*, Etibank), a relatively "small player" who was charged with defrauding his own bank out of a mere $1.2 billion.

According to Aydın Doğan, the media mogul who controls more than half of the print circulation in Turkey, of the ten families held responsible for the banking collapse and the fiscal crisis of 2001, five were media bosses. He accused them of blackmailing and terrorizing state institutions so they would not suffer the consequences of their actions which defrauded the Turkish treasury out of a total of $25 to $30 billion.

Of the three media barons who ended up in the hot seat, the Uzan Group collapsed under the enormous weight of the network of corruption they had constructed. But Mehmet Emin Karamehmet played his hand masterfully. He continued to exert pressure on the regime through his media outlets, while threatening to disrupt the banking system through various legal maneuvers. Fearing a run on both of his banks, the government caved in and allowed Karamehmet to repay his debts in fifteen years at an interest rate of 1.95 percent. Considering that the treasury was borrowing at an annual interest rate of 11 percent, the generosity of the government represented an extra burden of $4 billion for the Turkish taxpayers.

The picture is not complete unless we remind ourselves that the Doğan Media Group too had gone knocking at the door of the government. Through a partnership with Iş Bankası, the largest private bank in the country, the Doğan Media Group had acquired, from the State Board of Privatization, 51 percent of the shares of the state-owned petroleum distribution company POAŞ (Petrol Ofisi Anonim Şirketi) for $1.2 billion. Now Doğan Media needed help to adjust and reschedule the payments of the loan. The government, once again, happily obliged.

These captains of a so-called independent media were now at the mercy of the very power they were supposed to monitor and criticize. The reaction by the various media outlets reflected the fault lines of the industry and showed, once again, that every time the press makes compromises, the biggest loser is the truth. One of *Sabah*'s columnists, E. Babahan, on the morning of October 13, 2003, called the rescheduling "the real waterspout!" (For some time, the term "waterspout" had become synonymous with fraudulent actions that sucked all the funds out of a bank and transferred them to the owner's overseas accounts.) The next day, Doğan Group's flagship papers returned the insult: "The crooks who caused the bankruptcy of the State Treasury have now become slanderers!" The exchanges continued, with increasing animosity and vitriol, for a good ten days.

If the loser was the truth and the good name of independent journalism, there was no doubt as to who the winner was. Now the Islamist administration had the media barons right where it wanted them to be. It was a dark day indeed for transparent, honest, independent journalism. Newspapers had become docile house pets of the government, either aggressively partisan or timid for fear of offending the ruling powers.

◆　　　◆　　　◆

And what about the columnists? Were they expected to toe the company line? The usual argument to refute the above question originated from none other than the managing editor of *Hürriyet*, Ertuğrul Özkök. On numerous occasions, he has pointed out that among the columnists writing for the daily *Hürriyet* are some who espouse ideological thoughts diametrically opposed to those of others working for the same paper. That is quite true, but the reality of the Turkish media is a lot different than that of the American or the French press.

Three features of a Turkish newspaper distinguish it from those of other countries. First, without exceptions, Turkish papers do not carry an editorial page reflecting the collective position of its editorial staff on the burning issues of the day. For example, they will not openly declare who they support in a particular electoral race. This leads to some dishonest and corrupt media practices such as manipulating the news by omission or by commission or by outright fabrication.

Second, Turkish papers are a cross between a reputable opinion paper and a tabloid worthy of Fleet Street. Some of the most erudite and wise columnists you will ever read share the page with scandal-sheet gossipers. While in Europe, I take special care while reading my morning Turkish papers. Indeed a man would be wise to do some creative blockage of the back pages of most of these papers lest he leaves the impression of a "dirty old man."

Finally, the media culture, with its personal attacks even among the columnists of the same paper, does not lend itself to the development of "opinion makers." The force of persuading the public is left to the judgment of the editor and the *mise-en-page* of the paper.

In my estimation, Turkish newspapers must be some of the world's largest consumers of color print. Rather than lead their readership and raise their level of appreciation of the written word, they, much like their political counterparts, seek the lowest common denominator and try to sell dreams instead of ideas. In doing so, they add to the pollution created by dumbed-down TV programs.

We saw a clear example of how the news can be manipulated, either by commission or by omission, in the Malatya orphanage scandal. When this major item broke, news of the abuses did appear on all of the major evening news broadcasts, and yet not even a single column appeared in the front pages of three of the major dailies (*Vakit, Milli Gazete, Yeni Asya*), all rabid supporters of Islamist causes and of the regime. In another major daily (*Yeni Şafak*), which not only supports the regime but whose columnists, on occasion, outright endorse it, the news was reported, but the headlines made it seem as though the previous governments were responsible for the abuse of the children. These dailies proved that omitting a news item is sometimes as effective as distorting it.

◆   ◆   ◆

Another unique feature of the Turkish print media is the sight of columnists engaging in deadly serious polemic, sometimes even with others writing for the same paper. And the language can sometimes hit well below the belt. Turkish intelligentsia has a proclivity to devour each other, says Elif Safak (*Turkish Daily news,* December 4, 2005) She goes on further and declares that Turkish intelligentsia is famous for their hostility and cruelty towards one another: "We are a small cultural elite wherein musicians condemn other musicians and authors condemn other authors."

◆   ◆   ◆

In the world of Turkish media, a most serious insult, would find parallels between the targeted individual and the media collaborators of yesteryears.

Indeed, at the end of World War I, during the occupation of Istanbul by the Allied Forces, the most venomous term that one could hurl at those who opposed Mustafa Kemal and his insurrection and advocated some form of accommodation, protection, or mandate, if not outright surrender, in order to secure the future of the throne and of the Caliphate, was to label them as the "armistice media" or the media of "surrender." Others would refer to such writers as "pro-mandate" (*mandacı*). Nowadays, media who accept the European Union's demands, particularly ones that are humiliating and potentially harmful to the unitary nature of the Turkish state, are given the old "collaborationist" label. And I will be the first to plead *mea culpa* to the use of the term *mandacı*. Is this unfair? The question is not one that can be answered easily, and the responsibility for it must rest partly on the shoulders of those who, for several years, worked in Turkey representing the European Commission. Their hands were not too clean.

The ire of some was directed particularly towards Karen Fogg, who for four years (1998–2002) served in Ankara as European Commission's head of delegation. When some of her e-mail communications were intercepted and published, the reaction was "I told you so!" (Doğu Perinçek, *Karen Fogg'un E-Postalları*, Kaynak Yayınları 2002)

Karen Fogg, in her communications, had used code words to refer to certain institutions and personalities. She had used a "T," probably for Turkey. "Sleeping Beauties", in all likelihood, stood for "collaborationist forces" and "Sleeping Dogs" for the armed forces or maybe the president, to whom she also referred as HoR (head of republic) in many other compromising notes and messages. These e-mail messages supported the argument of those who maintained all along that the European Commission was manipulating the Turkish policy centers by pulling the strings of high bureaucrats, influential businessmen, NGOs, and fat cats—but especially media personalities. Some in the media were easy prey, ready to do the dirty work for the highest bidder. Turkish media must have been a fertile ground for yellow journalism, and now some had found a generous paymaster.

However, the above is a far cry from the irresponsible and unsubstantiated accusation hurled at the media by none other than the minister of foreign affairs and vice premier Abdullah Gül who accused the media of being receptive to the manipulations of foreign services and diplomats (*Hürriyet*, February 22, 2006). The negative effects of the government's dilly-dallying and its disingenuous attitude regarding the Hamas visit had created such a firestorm that it was time to divert the public's attention from the main issue to something Gül was good at. Indeed, in the fall of 2003, while serving as prime minister, he was reported to

have accused the media of having sold their services to U.S. interests for the purpose of influencing Turkish public opinion in support of a military action against
Iraq. He denied having made such an accusation.

Such insults and accusations have frequently been among the weapons used
during media wars. Pro-government media joined the Foreign Minister Gül in
accusing those opposed to certain government actions of being hired by Israeli
and U.S. secret services. *Yeni Şafak,* for example, has given notice that if and
when the government decides against the purchase of U.S. Arrow missiles, those
who would dare criticize the decision will be branded as agents of the foreign services of Israel and of the U.S.

Others in the media, masquerading today as conservative, pro-Islamist, and
pro-European Unionist, have had a checkered past. Old leftists, even unapolo-
getic Maoists of yesteryears, have now moved on and are happily drinking from
the trough set up by their new media barons. The amen corner of this media certainly deserved to be called "the best pen money can buy!" Their vanity, greed,
and cowardice to the pressures of state power (or to the profit motive of their
bosses) caused them to become the pollutants of a free and democratic press.
Here is how one fearless and honest voice aptly describes the present-day Turkish
media:

> Turkish media has ignored the beating taken by the republic, by the reforms
> of Mustafa Kemal, and instead it has supported this regime, like a business-
> man would, solely by paying attention to the rate of the dollar and the trend
> of the stock market. And yet the media should have known that nothing can
> be achieved by relying upon a medieval culture and by practicing religious
> exploitation. The media must be more intelligent, more alert, more secular,
> and more pro-contemporary Turkey than anybody else. The media should
> have known that one cannot advance forward in the company of reactionaries.
> (Bekir Coşkun, *Hürriyet,* February 25, 2006)

Reactionary, anti-republican, anti-secular papers have, in the past, played a
rather sordid role in orchestrating attacks against secular republicans. Back in
1995, one rabid advocate of political Islam, the religious paper *Akit* had provided
the name and picture of the President of Gümüşane Bar Association and had
made him the target of religious fanatics. He was later murdered in his office.

The very same publication—its name since changed to *Vakit*-did it again in
early 2006. Under a banner headline "These are the judges!" the religious paper
published the names and photos of the judges of the second chamber of the High
Court for Administrative Justice (Danıştay). It had taken a judicial decision bar-

ing the promotion of a headmistress wearing the Muslim headscarf. Three months later they were falling victim to shooting by a gunman, himself a lawyer,

◆   ◆   ◆

But in addition to issues that could potentially corrupt or distort the news-reporting aspect of the media, there are others just as critical. For example, there is the excessive entanglement of print and electronic media. In the United States, major columnists are seldom regulars on television. Shields and Brooks on the *Lehrer News Hours*, David Broder on *Meet the Press* and the few others who appear in both media are rarities. But on Turkish television, the big names of the print media all have regular talk shows. And securing a prominent politician to appear on one of these shows is extremely newsworthy. Politicians are quite aware of the favor they are doing when they appear on such programs for a full hour, one on one. They will be especially receptive to such invitations if they know they will receive softball questions that will allow them to hit a few home runs. Reporters known to ask hard-hitting questions will have a hard time finding a politician willing to submit to his or her grilling. I watched several appearances by the PM on a program called *One-on-One* (*Teke Tek*). The journalist, Fatih Altaylı, is a controversial host, but the deference with which he treated the Prime Minister seemed to me a bit exaggerated. Furthermore, by giving the Prime Minister a podium from which to reach millions, and appear regal while doing so (which is very important in the traditional Turkish custom), Fatih Altaylı became a silent partner of the powerful. For that, he was even rewarded by the PM, who presented him with one of his family pets. It was natural, therefore, that he created quite a stir when he parted with his old employer, *Hürriyet*, and joined *Hürriyet*'s arch enemy and main competitor, *Sabah*. Why did this happen? I suspect it was because he lost his prime-time perch on one of Doğan Media's main TV channels.

In the symbiotic world of print and electronic media, the players are rarely active at only one level. Other major columnists with their own shows are very good at lobbing soft questions to the rich and powerful. These include Taha Akyol, an intellectual voice of the far right, and Ismet Berkan, who masquerades as a liberal but in truth is a sworn enemy of anything remotely associated with Kemalism. In fact, oddly enough, Özkök (*Hürriyet*), Akyol (*Milliyet*), and Berkan (*Radikal*) are all employed by the Doğan Media Group.

At the other end of the spectrum, one finds several big hired guns among the religious right's papers too. Some of them speak with such an air of authority that you would suspect they were representative for the Islamist regime. One of them is Fehmi Koru, who on occasion will use the pseudonym "Taha Kıvanç."

The regime routinely uses local media to defend its policies, especially when the challenges originate abroad. However, sometimes local fat cats can corral the international media in order to pursue their own business interests. A case in point is an article that appeared in the *Washington Times* (September 27, 2005). After it sent alarm bells throughout the capital, Taha Kıvanç decided to look into the matter by inquiring about the motives of those who would call the present regime "Islamo-fascist" (*Yeni Safak*, September 30 and October 5, 2005). And lo and behold, what do we have here? Some familiar names of the rich and the corrupt, such as Mustafa Süzer and Murat Demirel...T. Kıvanç's articles, specifically, focus on Mustafa Süzer whose Kentbank was seized by the administration. And the articles proudly announce that the enemies of the Islamist regime have been identified: they are a Washington cabal bent on pressuring the Turkish government into returning Kentbank to its previous owner! According to Kıvanç this sinister group of neo-conservatives includes Robert Pollock, Michael Rubin, and Frank J. Gaffney Jr. along with the "Prince of Darkness" Richard Perle. And the story of Richard Perle dining at the Süzer-owned Ritz-Carlton is Kıvanç's final clue to decipher the mystery of this Washington-inspired assault on the Islamist regime.

But perhaps the real moral of this story is that fat cat crooks who know how to "take care" of the bank deposits of their customers are canny enough to know how to hire international hit men to serve their interests. Who knows? Maybe Süzer thought if it can be done in Turkey, it could be done elsewhere.

◆   ◆   ◆

For over a decade, the battle for the attention of the Turkish reader—and now the Turkish viewer as well—has been waged between two giants groups: Doğan and Sabah. The sad reality is that the public's sole source of information is tainted, and unreliable. The financial resources at the disposal of the religious right are such that the media outlets controlled by the Islamists are just as manipulative and monopolistic as the rest.

Up until the Islamists took power, the right wing religious media was a major voice of opposition against the Republican "system." Then, suddenly, they became "their master's voice," a modified version of the "official gazette." As for the Kemalists, the Republican forces, and the leftist intelligentsia, they are a tiny minority when it comes to reaching readers. And we may have to wait a long time before they reach the prime-time viewer.

However, during the past decade, the most corrosive influence has been that of the EU, exerted through its surrogates. They can be shrewd, canny, and misleading—all the while appearing as solid defender of the national interest. Lately, a tired old voice from the amen corner of the EU offered a new euphemism for a regime most would easily recognize as an elegant way of describing an EU administered territory (in blunt Turkish 'manda') : "From Turkey's angle," thundered Hasan Cemal, "the EU is the best umbrella." (*Milliyet*, November 30, 2005) It appears that Karen Fogg's spirit is alive and well in the media towers dotting the skyline of Istanbul. Furthermore, the terrorist organization PKK has made successful inroads into the European Union bureaucracy and through their agents has managed to manipulate some of the big guns of the media. They have become prime apologists for the political wing of the PKK, all under the guise of protecting the so-called democratic advances of the past few years. There is an almost one to one correlation between those advocating EU dependence and those pushing for de-facto recognition of the political wing of the PKK. Mehmet Ali Birand, Hasan Cemal, Güneri Cıvaoglu are some of such major players. They will mostly sing the Iraki Kurdish leader M. Barzani's tune.

Another characteristic typical of Turkish writers is their unbridled enthusiasm when given the opportunity to appear in the European media. Celebrated novelist Orhan Pamuk, during an interview with a Swiss newspaper, commented that a million and a half Armenians and thirty thousand Turkish-Kurds have been murdered and no one in Turkey dares admit to it. He then boasted that he was not afraid to call it like it is, or rather like it was. The prosecutor promptly charged him with defamation of the nation. The case was subsequently dismissed.

The episode reflects several fault lines within the Turkish political, literary, and social bodies. At one level, there seems to be a consensus that the article of the penal code under which Orhan Pamuk was charged is a confusing piece of legislation in need of change. That it was dictated by the commissars of the EU Commission lends a bit of comedic irony to the whole affair. However, on the other hand, there seems to be an equally strong sentiment against Orhan Pamuk due to the unsubstantiated nature of his claims. He later claimed to have been misquoted, but then changed his mind and said he stood by his words. More recently, prior to his first day of appearance before the court, in an article he wrote for the NewYorker magazine, he claimed he was making "the case for true Western democracy in [his] part of the world." (*The New Yorker*, December 19,

2005). Where and how he was making the case for Western democracy in his corner of the world was left to the imagination of the readers.

I am inclined to subscribe to the Italian novelist Giuseppe Montesano's advice. In an interview with a French daily (*Le Monde,* December 23, 2005), he suggested, "A writer ought to get involved in politics through his books, not by what he tells to people around him." Yet, Orhan Pamuk, until some of his late work, refused to deal with the burning issues of the Turkish society within which he operates, whereas another great novelist, Yaşar Kemal, has a body of work that consists of great novels, each confronting the reader with the daily human tragedies of Anatolia and its people. Of course, Pamuk, essentially an Istanbul writer who still lives in the neighborhood where he was born, lacked the perspective Kemal could bring to such issues.

◆　　　◆　　　◆

The fallout of this story is even more revealing than the story itself. Some self-anointed "intellectual" writers signed a petition for the abolition of the article under which Pamuk was charged. And yet, at about the same time, an even more serious breach of the law was being committed in the east, where the president of the University of Van was incarcerated for seventy-five days on trumped-up charges. But he, being a true son of the Kemalist era, was not one the intellectuals of the religious right, the fellow travelers of the PKK, and the Marxists and Maoists of the extreme left could, nor wanted to, care for.

A signatory to the petition and a self-declared member of this so-called "cultural elite" or "intelligentsia," Elif Şafak had no inhibitions about mocking the state as an "exquisite republic founded by Atatürk" and the Kemalists as "the guardians of the hegemony." (*Turkish Daily News*, December 4, 2005) To understand the depth of her animosity towards this "exquisite" republic, one needs to read her interview with Khatchig Mouradian ("On Bruises, Beauties, and Makeup," www.*aztagdaily.com*) and the details of her presentation at UCLA during a conference called "Three Turkish Voices on the Ottoman Armenians," organized by the UCLA Armenian Education Foundation Chair and reported in "Life in the Armenian Diaspora" (November 7, 2005, www.*cilicia.com*). The three academics, Elif Şafak, Taner Akçam, and Fatma Müge Göçek, are at the forefront of an intense coast-to-coast campaign, including appearances during the April 17 remembrance day, for all practical purposes, to certify the genocidal action of the Ottoman armies. In an interview she had with Khatchig Mouradian ("On the Foundations of Turkey" www.*aztagdaily.com)*, Müge Göçek gives the rationale for her interest in the subject matter: "The way that the Armenians came into the picture had to do with my particular location in the U.S." Michigan is in fact a state with a large Armenian community, but she went further, explaining her involvement by referring to her pursuit of academic tenure: "Initially, the issue was extremely politicized for me to venture into that field…and after I established my professional standing here and got tenure…" It is a fact that taking up positions favorable to powerful lobbies, be they in Europe or in the U.S., can have very rewarding consequences for writers, academics, and even artists. The reverse is equally true.

According to Müge Göçek, Turkey will recognize the Armenian genocide by the year 2015, at about the time of its projected accession to the EU.

◆   ◆   ◆

The Ottoman—Armenian tragedy of 1880–1919 has, recently, taken center stage in the Turkish media. The efforts of Armenian lobbies, in Europe and in North America, to force Turkey to recognize the tragedy as "genocide" has created quite a resentment throughout Turkey. According to Günay Evinch ("The Armenian Cause in America Today," *Turkish Policy Quarterly*, February 23, 2006) WWI took the lives of 10 million combatants and 50 million civilians. In eastern Anatolia alone, over one million Muslims—mostly Kurds, Turks, and Arabs—and almost 600,000 Armenians perished. The Ottoman Empire lost over five million of her citizens, of which 4 million were Muslim, 600,000 were Armenian, 300,000 were Greek, and 100,000 were Ottoman Jewish. As to whether the atrocities constitute genocide, Evinch is quite explicit. She recognizes the fact that each side views the same historical events and yet reaches opposite conclusions. The Armenians have all along maintained that the Ottoman government acted as they did driven by a desire to destroy them as an ethnic or religious group. Thus the tragedy is genocide. The Armenian reluctance to admit that there have been massive losses of lives on the Muslim side may be due ignorance but more likely to being in denial. However, the implication of Armenian responsibility in the deaths of the Muslims has always been the main point of contention. And yet that is an issue historians have long addressed.

As for the Turkish position, it has consistently rejected the genocide argument. For the Turks the historical events that caused massive human losses are: i) the large scale revolt by the Armenian Revolutionary Federation Army 1880–1919; ii) the Armenian spearheaded Russian invasion of eastern Anatolia in 1915; iii) the Ottoman crackdown on Armenian rebel leaders and related relocation of Armenian civilians from the eastern war zones in 1915; iv) the Armenian spearheaded French invasion of southern Anatolia in 1917–19; v) fighting between Armenian and Muslim villages for domination of the eastern and southern provinces; vi) disease and starvation.

According to Evinch, Armenian non-governmental organizations have dedicated vast resources to what is referred to, in Armenian, as *Hai Tahd*, or the "Armenian Cause." It includes three policy objectives: (1) recognition that the Armenian deaths constituted genocide, (2) reparations from Turkey, and (3) restitution of the eastern provinces of Turkey to Armenia. And yet, the Armenian position is to oppose the idea of a court decision as to whether the Armenian case constitutes genocide. This position has been expressed openly by Armenian Foreign Minister Vardan Oskanian and is supported by scholar Samantha Powers, who specialized on the mass killings in Rwanda. She maintains that the legislative and public-relations approach promises to be a more successful route toward a moral—if not legal—conviction of Turkey and the people of Turkey. Given the fact that, under the UN convention, genocide is a crime that can only be determined by the International Court of Justice at the Hague or by domestic courts of member states that have laws against genocide, the Armenian reluctance to take the issue to court and opt to take the politically expedient route is rather revealing as to the merit of their case.

It is clear, by now, that the issue of genocide will be debated before the public, not in courts. Winning the attention and the approval of the masses for the Turkish case requires a significant amount of work. The Armenian lobby is a very efficient and powerful political machine. The three Turkish scholars, whatever their motivations and whatever historical evidence they have at their disposal, are certainly an effective public-relation tool for the Armenian cause.

The surprising aspect of this issue is that the Turkish case is nowhere in sight.

◆　　◆　　◆

One can safely state that not much has changed over the past century in the attitude of the Turkish state when it comes to making its case and presenting historical facts and figures. The government's inability to defend itself against the charge of genocide is a mirror image of its incompetence when dealing with Turkey's contemporary problems. The problems are monumental in both cases: a governing elite incapable of putting the nation's vital interests ahead of their own; an economic and social landscape unfriendly to those less fortunate; bankrupt public finances coupled with a monumental public debt, all serving to undermine the growth of GDP, the expansion of employment; and a foreign policy ready and willing to capitulate to international lobbies and powers.

Under such circumstances, it is inevitable that a society pulverized by several decades of massive unemployment becomes Balkanized and centrifugal forces take over. As a result, a well-organized debate regarding the measures Turkey must adopt to develop a coherent vision of the future becomes improbable. What is needed is the lifting of the veil of demagogic rhetoric—which successive governments have employed via the media to convince the nation that prosperity and full employment was "just around the corner"—and instead an honest explanation to the nation of the unsustainable character of the present economic model, which condemns the youth and future generations to unemployment, middle-class families to pauperization, the least fortunate segments of the society to massive debts in the future.

Thus, it is imperative for the nation to realize that no viable solution is possible within the present system.

But how? Certainly not through a media whose captains, with Schengen visas in their pockets, spend most of their free time hop-scotching around the playgrounds of Europe, from Lake Como where one will search for a woman's fear of losing her lover, to the Maison des trois thés of Place Monge in Paris, where another will look for Lapsang Souchong tea! And obviously not in a Parliament where a coalition of "me first" deputies with deep pockets are too busy lining them. The political, business, and intellectual classes seem unable to put their gray cells to use developing social, economic, and political master plans and offering them, with conviction, to a nation in search of a light—any light—at the end of the tunnel.

6

SILENT CAPITULATIONS: A ROAD TO PERDITION

The term "capitulations," in Turkish historical context, is truly an ugly word. It immediately brings to mind the abject surrender, during the late Ottoman era, of state sovereignty in legal, economical, and fiscal matters.

Today, many observers of the Turkish scene will not hesitate to charge the current regime of going down the same slippery slope and surrendering the prerogatives of the Republic to foreign interests. Remarkably however, the proponents of the present economic policy, the claque that never misses a chance to applaud the government's actions, have also dared to use the "C" word lately. Indeed, in an article critical of a deal that led to the delivery of natural gas across the Black Sea (from Russia to Turkey, called the "Blue Stream"), Ismet Berkan states, "Secret treaties were signed with Russia...and special privileges were accorded to the Russian gas company in terms equivalent to capitulations, and these terms have become part of the law." (*Radikal*, January 3, 2006) What we don't know, of course, is whether his reaction would have been so negative (and whether he would have used the "C" word), had the deal been struck during this administration's tenure or if the transaction had involved the European Union or any of its major companies. One thing is certain: Karen Fogg would not have approved of it.

◆　　　◆　　　◆

In the valley of the Orkhon River, in northern Mongolia, there are two large monuments that were erected in the eighth century in honor of the Turkish prince Kul and his brother, the emperor Bilge Khaghan. On one of them, it is written:

"If the sky above did not collapse and if the earth below did not give way, oh, Turk people, who could destroy your state and your institutions?"

Indeed, since 732 A.D., the Turkish nation and state faced annihilation and extinction on several occasions, and the most recent threat is just as serious as some previous ones—namely, the "European Union" and its "criteria." The negotiating framework document adopted by the EU Council on October 3, 2005, is a document that in many ways codifies a relationship that can exist only between a master and its servant. Here is why this is so:

- The term "open ended," which was never uttered prior to or during negotiations with any other candidate country, appears to have been coined solely for the purpose of reassuring the public in member countries where very large majorities oppose Turkish membership.

- A demand regarding what the EU defines as national minorities is totally contrary to the republic's founding charter and the Treaty of Lausanne. It constitutes additional evidence that the EU is determined to humiliate Turkey during the course of the negotiations. In fact:

  - Turkey has been put on notice that, even if admitted, her citizens may not enjoy indefinitely the full rights and privileges of membership, such as freedom of movement;

  - By calling on Turkey to accept the *acquis* of the union, including acts, legally binding or not, adopted within the union framework (such as inter-institutional agreements, resolutions, statements, and recommendations), the playing field has been tilted towards the interests of the union members by bringing in the role of the European Parliament which passed some resolutions of its own capable of dynamiting the whole process. Such as:

    - The European Parliament's call on the Commission to fully assess, by the end of 2006, the implementation of the extended Ankara Agreement regarding the Customs Union between Turkey and the EU, with its implication of an unequivocal Turkish recognition of the Republic of Cyprus

    - The European Parliament's call on Turkey to recognize the Armenian genocide as a prerequisite for accession to the EU

Given the hurdles ahead and the traps set for her, the best deal Turkey can expect at the end of the accession process is "second class" status, an inelegant way of saying "privileged partnership."

Economically, socially, politically, and in the international arena, Turkey is acting like an "addict" whose dependency on the European Union directives are beginning to affect her social fabric, her international standing, and her economic future. Yet Europe, as we have known it, is failing. According to Britain's former Minister for Europe, Douglas Alexander, "There is remarkably little evidence that European loyalties are replacing national loyalties." He reminds us that "armies stay national and people are increasingly focused on national identities." As for the future of social policies, he underlines the point that there is "certainly no iron rule that suggests that collective European action is more effective than national action in delivering social justice."

Even when, all over the old and the new Europe, loss of confidence in the European Union model and its market economy is in the air, Turkey's Islamists will not take a single step without consulting with their future masters. Today, due to the absence of an effective social security safety net, millions of Turks and their families are marginalized by unemployment. The remedy—investments in national infrastructure projects—is at the mercy of an IMF-directed budget, which calls for a 6 to 6.5 percent surplus in order to accommodate the financial lords of the world.

◆   ◆   ◆

For several decades, the tendency of the Turkish establishment has been to adopt internal and external policies appropriate for a "client state," ignoring all the associated risks and dangers. The fat cats of the business elite have always joined, if not guided, the political elite and, together, like an ostrich, they have seen only what they wanted to see and ignored flashing danger signals. When, not long ago, the former German Chancellor Helmut Schmidt said, "Failure to dismantle Turkey following the Treaty of Sevres was a major blunder," or when, former French president Giscard d'Estaing was just as blunt in declaring, "Those who do support Turkey's EU membership are the enemies of the European Union," Teflon-coated Turkish leaders closed their eyes and shut their ears, hoping that nothing would stick on them or on their policies. Unfortunately for them, reality proved hard to ignore, and now it has come to haunt them in the form of German Chancellor Angela Merkel and French Interior Minister and potential presidential candidate Nicholas Sarkozy, who have added their voices to the chorus that will eventually force Turkey to accept ignominiously the glorified status of "privileged partnership."

In its latest report, *Turkey: 2005 Progress Report* (November 9, 2005), the European Commission called on Turkey to take meaningful steps concerning its Customs Union obligations. The report demands that Turkey ensure non-discriminatory treatment of EU bidders, avoid discrimination against EU goods and suppliers, and lift restrictions in competition. Remarkably, nowhere in the report is there any hint that the EU will consider leveling the playing field by removing quotas against Turkish agricultural goods. Forcing Turkey to open its internal market to EU goods while denying her the means to pay for those goods is a throwback to colonialist practices of old, which Europe practiced only too well and for too long.

In a country where, according to World Bank's 2006 Development Report, 4.8 percent of the population—about 3.5 million Turks—survive on an income of one dollar a day (based on purchasing power parity), no government policy that fails to address the nation's overarching interests can be carried out, even if such policy is advocated by the European Union, the IMF, or the World Bank. Yet, successive governments have shamelessly surrendered the nation's sovereignty regarding the national budget to multinational authorities. Let's look at some of the hot issues that have the potential to derail the accession talks:

1. How can the Turkish Parliament and the Turkish government admit that genocide was committed against the Armenians during WWI?

Historian Justin McCarthy makes a compelling case about the true nature of that conflict:

> The conflict between Muslims and Armenians of the Ottoman East, which had been developing for a hundred years, came to a climax during World War I. Two wars were fought at the same time in the east—a war between Ottoman and Russian armies and an inter-communal war between Armenians and Muslims of eastern Anatolia and the southern Caucasus. In terms of civilian and military losses, the wars fought in the east between 1914 and 1920 were among the worst in human history. The result of Ottoman weakness, Russian imperialism, European meddling, and Armenian revolutionary nationalism was widespread devastation. After the wars, cities such as Van, Bitlis, Bayazıt, and Erzincan were largely rubble.
>
> Thousands of villages were destroyed. Millions on both sides had died. The Armenians, who revolted to gain a nation, were left with a Soviet republic in which they were not their own masters. The Turks, who ultimately won the

wars, were left with a country in ruins. (Justin McCarthy, *Death and Exile: The Ethnic Cleansing of Ottoman Muslims, 1821–1922,* 1995)

While referring to a recent conference held at Bilgi University, in Istanbul, in late September 2005, on the subject of Ottoman-Armenian conflict, the European Commission reported that "[the conference] was held with the participation of different viewpoints."(*Turkey: 2005 Progress Report,* November 9, 2005) This, of course, is untrue! In fact, the organizers made doubly sure that only EU's hired hands would be invited. That sort of distorted reporting of the facts casts serious doubts on the objectivity of the Commission. It seems that the spirit of Karen Fogg is alive and well in the halls of EU's Brussels headquarters.

No EU resolution, no European Parliament amendment, no European Commission—hired marionettes will be able to alter the judgment of history. And, certainly, a nation that has honored her martyrs and heroes for centuries will not now, turn around and, dishonor them.

2. What Turkish government will go willingly against the national consensus that has emerged since 1974 regarding the future of Turkish Cypriots and that of their Republic?

Following the referendum regarding the Annan Plan, the Turkish government and Turkish Cypriots had nothing to show for their cooperation, whereas the Greek Cypriots who rejected it not only paid no price but were rewarded with EU membership. The critics of the Turkish stance regarding the extension of the customs union to the new member states point to a political and legal paradox of not recognizing a member of a union to which Turkey is a candidate for adhesion. However, these same critics should remember the political and legal paradox of ignoring the guarantee that was provided to the communities and contracting parties by the 1960 treaties that constituted the bi-communal Republic of Cyprus. The treaties make it clear that the accession of the Republic of Cyprus to any international organization to which Turkey is not a member requires the consent of Turkey and of the Island's Turkish community. Furthermore, all three parties—the United Kingdom, Greece, and Turkey—guaranteed the fulfillment of this binding legal agreement. Any concession along these lines would severely undermine the regime's commitment to defending national interests.

Worse yet, history's judgment regarding the origins of this conflict will severely limit the nature of the compromises Turkish leaders will be able to make.

Let us review a few historical facts, best summarized in a letter dated January 2, 1968, from Rauf Denktaş, president of the Turkish Communal Chamber in Cyprus to the secretary general of the United Nations:

> As from December 1963, the Greek Cypriot Administrators have ceased to pay the salaries of all Turkish Cypriot Civil Servants, the Turkish Cypriot ministers and of the Vice-President of Cyprus and have thus attempted to leave the Turks of Cyprus without adequate means of administration while attacking individual Turkish villages or Turkish parts of the towns—on and off—with a view to forcing upon the Greek Cypriots the Greek Cypriot will of ENOSIS as a political settlement. Having rendered a deadly blow at the established order, calculated to bring the regime to an end by destroying all the vital guarantees of the independence and territorial integrity of Cyprus, the Greek Cypriot administrators have attempted to set up an illegal and unconstitutional "government" through a number of *faits accomplis*, always moving on the assumption that the chaos which they themselves had planned and welted entitled them to bypass the Constitution on the ground of "acts of necessity." Thus, the Turkish Community was left with two alternatives:1) to agree to be ruled by the illegal and unconstitutional "administration" which the Greek Cypriots had set up under a variety of pretexts, or 2) to defy this arbitrary rule which was being imposed on them by the gunmen of this so-called administration and to seek ways and means of keeping up the Constitutional order within all Turkish areas and for all Turkish Cypriots.

That, in a nutshell, is the birth of the Turkish Republic of Northern Cyprus. Any "sellout" of the Turkish Cypriot cause in exchange for a favorable outcome of the EU accession talks would indeed be a Faustian bargain!

3. What parliamentary majority can, in today's climate, abrogate the Treaty of Lausanne, confer on the Fener Patriarch Bartolomeos the ecclesiastical title of ecumenical patriarch, and go further by reopening the Heybeliada (Chalki) Greek Orthodox Seminary?

How can this even be considered when Athens still retains the unenviable record of being the lone European capital without a mosque and where, recently, five thousand Moslems had to celebrate the feast of Ramadan, on a rainy day, in the corridors of a football stadium? It is worth remembering that the problems faced by the Turkish minority in Western Thrace continue to be a disgrace for the host country. The day Turkish leaders begin tinkering with articles of the Treaty of Lausanne, would be "a day of infamy" indeed.

4. How can the government justify the retrial or the reopening of the case of Abdullah Öcalan, given that thousands of parents and relatives are still mourning the death of their loved ones—innocent, unarmed victims murdered in cold blood in the dead of night? How can the government acquiesce to the demand of the European Commission, which keeps emphasizing the urgency of reopening this case?

The European Commission's recommendations regarding the problems in Southeastern Turkey are based on a series of misdiagnoses, and the remedies are thus substantially faulty. The European Commission believes that if the Turkish state recognizes the ethnic identity of its Kurdish citizens as a minority, and if the Kurds secure true representation in Parliament through electoral reform, the so-called Kurdish problem will be partly resolved. But the cold reality is that Southeast Turkey suffers from the persistence of a tribal culture, with feudal chiefs and drug lords dominating the social and political scene. Without a genuine social revolution, land reform, the education and empowerment of women and the end of violence perpetrated against women the picture will not change.

The issue of equitable representation in Parliament cannot be advanced until the tribal chiefs' grip on all facets of life within the society is forever broken. However, this is impossible in the present system, as the MPs in Parliament who currently represent the Southeast are tribal chiefs or members of a tribal chief's family.

In reality, Turkey has no Kurdish problem—she has a problem caused by a feudal system, the antithesis of a functioning democracy; she has a problem caused by a tribal culture, an anachronism in the twenty-first century; she has a problem caused by a patriarchal culture that denigrates women, denying them their rightful place in the society and erecting barriers to their empowerment. Politicians who speak as if a functioning democracy is possible there without first overcoming the debilitating influences of this triple threat are lying to the nation, and history will not be kind to such demagogues.

The complete implementation of the Kemalist agenda is a *sine qua non* condition for further social progress throughout Turkey. All previous right-of-center governments, as well as the current Islamist administration, have failed to grasp the significance of "women empowerment" in Turkey's effort to achieve the necessary level of contemporary civilization.

◆   ◆   ◆

Lately, the Prime Minister has brought into the picture a whole new concept. Reacting to riots and violence on the streets of Paris, he identified the cause of the rebellions: The ban of the Islamic headscarf! Was this a hint to the Turkish liberals? And a few days later, commenting on the possibility that the EU would refuse to admit Turkey, he openly stated that such a refusal would lead to a "war of civilizations." In saying so, he was explicitly admitting that Turkey belonged to the "other" camp. The Prime Mminister was even more uncomfortable following a recent verdict by the European Court of Human Rights, which stated in its ruling of November 10, 2005, that "there were extremist political movements in Turkey which sought to impose on the society as a whole their religious symbols and concept of a society founded on religious precepts."

Ironically, the Turkish communists and their allies, who in the seventies and eighties sought to create the "Turkish People's Republic," and the fanatics of the religious right, who want nothing less than the "Turkish Islamic Republic," have now joined forces and are clamoring for Turkey's entry into the European Union! The logic behind the union of these strange bedfellows is none other than their mutual enmity of the Kemalist forces. Each is willing to make common cause with the other whom they regard as the "snake," until the day when the commissars in Brussels will have to choose one or the other. But then, it will be too late for those who hoped for the day when Turkey may choose to enter the EU, not as a mendicant, but as a member with full rights and privileges.

Meanwhile, the outcome of Turkey's accession to the EU will have a profound effect on the lives of Mr. and Mrs. Muhacir & Halime Erüç, who live in the village of Meydandağı of the District of Patnos in the Province of Ağrı. According to the news service DHA (December 20, 2004), the Erüç family, with their twenty-seven children, are hoping for a financial windfall from the union of Europe and Turkey.

◆   ◆   ◆

The role played by the Turkish Armed Forces in the formulation of the state's overall strategic planning is an issue the EU is raising regularly. Over the years, that role has evolved, and it will continue to adapt and adjust to the maturing character of the Turkish society. However, the danger lies not so much in the incessant demands of the EU for civilian control over the military, but rather in the push to silence the military's input into the debate over the future direction of the Republic—including, but certainly not limited to, the degree of ongoing Islamization, the devolution of the state structures, and the atomization of the society into a multitude of minorities—in short, the efforts to end the Kemalist Republic as we have known it for over eighty years.

A recent article delved with the EU's effort to curb the military's influence in determining Turkey's strategic posture in the next decades. (Ersel Aydınlı, Nihat Ali Özcan, and Doğan Akyaz,"The Turkish Military's March toward Europe," *Foreign Affairs*, Jan/Feb 2006) Whether the authors were speaking with authority on behalf of the Turkish Armed Forces is questionable although the authors are affiliated with military institutions. However, the main theme of the article, that the Turkish Armed Forces, unable or rather unwilling to bite the bullet, would like to see the EU assume the primary role in solving Turkey's main social and political problems, deserves to be challenged. The authors' description of the EU as "a new guardian for [the] stability [...] of Turkey" borders on the insane. When will the Turkish Armed Forces relinquish their responsibilities and duties as "guardian of the republic" to outside powers? Furthermore, the statement "If, despite all the reforms, full membership does not materialize, it is Turkey's military, not its politicians, that will be left trying to hold together an even more fragmented country" is a polite way to admit that the Turkish Armed Forces are afraid to hold the bag lest they become a scapegoat during the ensuing debacle. I do not believe 'outsourcing' the defense of the country has ever been an option for the Turkish Armed Forces. Nor do I believe that the possibility of full membership not materializing is tantamount to a debacle.

But overall, the authors have missed a golden opportunity to highlight the risks involved in Turkey's EU adventure. Their reference to "the country's historic journey toward modernization" ignores the fact that without a revolutionary approach to eliminate a feudal and tribal culture, without educating future generations and provide them gainful employment, meeting the Copenhagen/Maastricht criteria would be equivalent to covering with a thick layer of cosmetic makeup the ugly façade of an irrelevant social, economic, and political establishment that is destined for the trash heap of history.

◆   ◆   ◆

The following op-ed article appeared in the May 7, 2004, issue of the *International Herald Tribune*.

Joining the EU: Membership Could Cost Turkey Its Soul

A former prime minister of Turkey, Mesut Yılmaz, declared in 1999 that "Turkey's road to the European Union goes through Diyarbakır," a mostly Kurdish city in Southeastern Turkey. He was alluding to European Union demands that Turkey grant more autonomy to its Kurdish citizens as the price of an eventual membership in the EU.

But a detour to Diyarbakır is not the only one that Turkey will be forced to take to win EU membership. The danger is that the journey will lead Turkey away from itself—making membership not worth the price, which is national sovereignty.

The demands on Turkey are many. Last January, Romano Prodi, the president of the EU Commission, intimated that the reunification of Cyprus would enhance Turkey's chances. With the Greek Cypriot electorate rejecting a reunification plan put forward by Kofi Annan, the UN secretary-general, it is now apparent that Turkey will continue to be pressured to offer more concessions to the Greek Republic of Cyprus to change its mind. In short, Turkey's road to the EU will have to pass through Nicosia too.

In addition, the United States wants Turkey to open its border with Armenia before the NATO summit meeting in Istanbul in June. Turkey closed the border more than a decade ago, when a war erupted between Armenia and Ankara's ally, Azerbaijan. Given the brittle nature of its economy and its dependence on the International Monetary Fund and World Bank, Turkey seems to have little choice but contemplate yet another detour to the EU, this time through Yerevan.

Finally, a failure to reach an agreement this year with Greece over territorial rights in the Aegean would lead to the World Court, as stipulated in the 1999 communiqué that officially named Turkey a candidate country. Thus Turkey's road to the EU may have to snake through The Hague too.

These issues all generate strong feelings among the Turks. They want Kurds treated as first-class citizens, for instance, but are deeply suspicious of any suggestion of autonomy. A strong urge for a fair and just partnership between the Greek and Turkish communities in Cyprus is tempered by memories of the terrorism by the Greek nationalist movement EOKA. And they fear that opening the Armenian border would be a betrayal of the Azeris who have been driven from their homes by Armenian troops.

With the EU planning to reconsider its status in December, Turkey is now faced with a historic decision: What price should the nation pay for just the promise of negotiations aimed at a future EU membership?

Unfortunately, a rational debate in Turkey about the pros and cons of EU membership has been clouded by a fog of disinformation. Big business conglomerates that control the news media are feverishly pushing for membership, while only a small handful of nationalist and leftist publications are daring to point out the problems with accession. Meanwhile, Turkey's Islamist regime seems to draw its legitimacy more from the praises of EU leaders, obsessed with the unification of Cyprus, or of the State Department, eager to assign to Turkey a major role in its new Greater Middle East project, than from the people.

Why are the government and businesses so intent on membership? The answer lies in Turkey's economic ills, including high unemployment and a monumental trade deficit attributable in part to a disadvantageous customs union with the EU. The underlying problem, however, is an unholy alliance between corrupt political elite that has sought to hang on to power by hook or crook and equally corrupt business elite that has robbed Turkey with the connivance of a meek, underpaid and sometimes crooked bureaucracy. To get itself out of this economic mess, the regime is banking on the generosity of a rather skeptical Europe.

But again, at what price? A country cannot be great without a strong sense of itself. Taking refuge in the bosom of the EU will not save Turkey unless it rediscovers its moral compass and refuses to surrender abjectly on matters of national interest. Turkey's road to the EU may well be its road to perdition.

In retrospect, today I can easily subscribe to each and every word I wrote in that article. Nothing has changed. In fact, events are evolving in a rather rapid pace and in a predictable direction. And it seems that, in the end, it will be the Europeans who will teach Turkey a bitter lesson about how not to surrender abjectly on matters of national interest.

◆   ◆   ◆

Turkish intellectuals continue to commit a critical error by equating the 1839 political reforms of Sultan Abdülmecid to the European Renaissance or to the Enlightenment, when in reality they were no more than poor imitations of what Europe was. In the post-Atatürk period, and to this day, no politician has given any indication that he has grasped the true nature of the challenge facing Turkey: educating and training broad-minded generations that are free of the cobwebs of superstition and old habits and ready to join the "contemporary civilization."

Indeed the overall picture is rather depressing:

- Foreign interests and multinational corporations have developed a stranglehold over the nation's political, economic and social life.

- Shipyards, ports, harbors, refineries, and steel mills are sold in the name of privatization. Foreign capital is purchasing functioning and profitable industries rather than investing in the establishment of new productive industries capable of generating employment for the million or more youth that is entering the work force each year.

- Millions are living below the poverty limit and many more are surviving at the edge of starvation.

- Seventy five percent of all industrial workers are paid the minimum wages and the condition of the textile workers is even worse.

- Social security is bankrupt.

- Public health services have been scuttled under the pressure of the International Monetary Union directives.

- Public education throughout the nation has been neglected in favor of private and religious schools.

- Millions of farmers have seen their subsidies eliminated due to pressure from the International Monetary Union directives. Their modest incomes will be further eroded when the government caves in to the European Union directives recommending drastic reductions in farm labor. Millions of farmers in search of work will contemplate migration to urban areas, thus contributing to the mushrooming of new slums around the big cities.

- The civil service has been politicized, and political cronies have been appointed to various government positions.

- The media is being controlled by major corporate moguls who seek to use their power to gain financial advantages for their far-flung business empires.

- Hot money and Arab capital, frozen out of the U.S. since 9/11, is chasing dirt-cheap real estate.

- The European Union, under the guise of accession negotiations, is gearing up to present to the Turkish government a list of requests and conditions totally inimical to the national interest.

- Certain segments of the population, encouraged by the government's Islamist policies, are hard at work to lay the foundations of the "second Republic."

- Others are working to dismantle the nation-state and lay the foundations of a confederation of Kurdish and Turkish states.

- The political elite, corrupt to the core and working in tandem with an equally corrupt corporate establishment, is trying to undo all the major social, political, and economic structures of the Kemalist past.

- While the nation is waiting for Godot, their leaders are striking a Faustian bargain, the outcome of which has never been in doubt.

This is the road to perdition. The road to salvation begins by taking a detour and adopting the philosophy and vision that formed the foundations of the Kemalist Republic. It calls for the same spirit that saved the nation in its darkest hours, the same vision that enabled the Republic to achieve great social reforms, same revolutionary zeal that established a secular system of governance, and a "for the people" agenda rather than a populist one.

EPILOGUE

The story of the rise and fall of empires is not a very original one. But the story of the birth of Kemalism is the story of courage, sacrifice, and vision.

Today, the political, social, and economic landscape of the country represents a rich man's jungle—an oligarchy of feudal lords, tribal chiefs, big business, and ruling political elite—in short, a system masquerading as a functioning democracy.

The truth is, the Turkish ruling establishment displays total indifference towards the law and utter disdain for the less fortunate members of the society. Submissiveness to the power of money, a lack of critical spirit, and an inability to distinguish the true from the false make these unfortunate souls easy prey for the powerful of the jungle. That we ask them to go to the polls once every five years seems to be enough to give the semblance of a democratic way.

The true nature of the present regime cannot be ascertained by simply listening to what they, themselves, claim to be. Those claims must be compared and, whenever possible, correlated with their deeds. And if the actions they have undertaken disprove their noble intentions, we must take note of that (even though we know that they are all "honorable men").

To illustrate, let's consider the recent outbreak of avian flu in the eastern part of Turkey and the ensuing reaction of the local people. For many Westerners, it is hard to comprehend the ignorance, poverty, and desolation of the villagers whose chickens had to be culled. As it was reported in the media, one man said: "Here, I have two wives, and I don't mind if you take both and throw them into the trash. But, please, I beg of you, do not take my chickens—they mean everything to me." (*Milliyet*, January 8, 2006). Another, an unemployed father living in a two-room house without running water and using an outhouse, lost two of his teenagers to the avian flu. He was honest but just as ignorant: "We ate the dead chicken, as before…Had we known better, we would have not eaten." (CNN-Türk) Another father, an equally miserable soul, has a sixteen-year-old daughter whom he has never allowed to go to school. Then, one day, when she is exposed to avian flu, her father shamelessly declares, "I have no social security, so if she is going to die, let her die here rather than in the hospital!"

The moral perversion and the morbid depravity buried in these few words should be food for thought. They are living examples of total and abject human poverty in a country that seems to have forgotten its less fortunate sons and daughters.

Turkish society needs a reminder that in today's world, a viable economy needs dependable institutions, fair and equitable laws, rules and regulations, a quality education accessible to all, sound research institutions, and an independent and honest judiciary, all working together for the "common good." The Turkish business establishment has a duty to prove that a free market is not just for the few but at the service of all. Moreover, they have to admit and accept that rules and regulations applied with firmness and fairness are essential to prevent the market from becoming a jungle. Should they fail to appreciate the seriousness of the issue, they will be the biggest losers. For inevitably the masses will become more and more aware of the inequalities and injustices.

◆   ◆   ◆

Two visions or rather two scenarios depicting the future course of Turkey are competing in my mind.

In one scenario, a man currently residing in the United States one day boards a plane and lands in Istanbul, where over two million of his supporters rush to the tarmac to greet him as the next savior of the nation. A Turkish version of the Iranian Islamic revolution, with all its symbolism, is about to be unfurled. Fethullah Gülen, the Turkish Khomeini, is about to meet with his followers. The Turkish Islamic Republic (or, as they like to call it, the "second Republic") is upon us!

In fact, for some, this is just a matter of time. Here is how Cengiz Çandar (*Bugün*, November 28, 2005), following a visit to Fethullah Gülen's 104-acre property nestled in the forests of Pennsylvania, puts it: "It is sad to note that the conditions for Fethullah Gülen's return to Turkey are not yet ripe as he continues to live the life of an émigré in exile!" I shudder to think how Turkey would look when the time is "ripe" for his return.

In the next scenario, another plane takes off from Moscow and lands in Istanbul with the remains of Nazım Hikmet, the greatest Turkish poet of the twentieth century, an avowed communist who was thrown in prison for writing revolutionary poems before escaping to Russia, where he died and was buried. His coffin is met by a quarter of a million of his admirors, who will take it to its final resting place without going through any of the usual rituals. It is the beginning of a series of "homecoming" events, including those of rebels who have wasted their youth in the mountains of Northern Iraq and Southeastern Turkey.

I am still an optimist. Why? I find the answer every night on the Internet sites through which I am forever connected to Turkey.

My hopes are high whenever I read a column of Bekir Coşkun, or Yiğit Bulut, Mine Kırıkkanat, Emin Çölaşan, Oktay Ekşi, Gündüz Aktan, Özdemir Ince, M. Ali Kışlalı, Güngör Mengi, Nuray Mert, the bubbly Ayşe Arman, and even Fatih Altaylı and Ertuğrul Özkök, among many others whom I admire and respect. They may not all believe in the Kemalist agenda, but they have the nation's best interests in mind. No renegade communists, no Karen Fogg/CIA/BND hired hands here. And the controversial intellect of Yalçın Küçük never ceases to amaze me. Especially when he dared to utter that the most ignorant person ever to govern Turkey, since Sultan Ibrahim (the insane), was the present Prime Minister I had to take note of it (Yalçın Küçük, *İsyan, v. 1,* İthaki Yayınları, 2005)

But I must admit that it was Ertuğrul Özkök, whom I criticized earlier for searching Lapsang Suchong tea in Paris, that had the best and most cogent article (*Hürriyet* May 18, 2006) dealing with the trauma and aftermath of the event he called "the 9/11 of Turkey." The simple yet devastating logic of his argument is breathtaking.

Özkök effectively contrasts the facts: i) Even though, to this date, no one has been killed in this land for being religious, many were murdered for being non-religious by thise who consider themselves pious; ii) Even though no one has been harassed or murdered for fasting, many have been routinely attacked for not fasting; iii) Even though no one has been mistreated for praying, in many Anatolian cities and towns people will take a jaundiced view of those who do not pray; iv) Even though no girl or woman has been assaulted for wearing a headscarf, those wearing miniskirts were not that lucky; v) Even though no one has been murdered in this land for being a Muslim cleric, a Christian cleric has been assassinated right in the middle of his church. He concludes: This country has a problem of religious fanaticism.

At another level, I am encouraged by the sight of young girls and women willing to stand up against the weight of tradition, tribe, and patriarchy and who desire to educate themselves. Women like Tuğba Karademir. No headscarf on her head! In fact, she did not care how covered her head or her legs were. But she skated like a true swan at the Winter Olympics in Torino, Italy. She represented the nation's youth with dignity and courage.

And then there is Hanefi Avcı. While security chief in Istanbul he successfully pursued and captured untold criminals, religious terrorists, and the Mafiosi. His hardline posture against the religious terrorists must have made the administration a bit uncomfortable so he was exiled to Edirne, a city on the northwest corner of the land, a gateway to Europe. There, once again, he proved that he had not lost an iota of his determination to fight corruption. By successfully placing hidden cameras at customs houses, he managed to catch more than fifty security and customs officers in the act of pocketing bribes from travelers.

◆   ◆   ◆

Or perhaps I found the answer in the story of Ç. C., a young Anatolian high school senior. On May 25, 2005, during Milas High School's Poetry Night (sponsored by the school's Department of Literature and held before an audience of more than 200 parents and dignitaries), the seventeen-year-old, who had already won a "best actor" award at a Theater Festival, defied his schoolmaster and complained that although students had organized the event, they were not allowed to read the poems of their choice. So, as master of ceremonies, he informed the audience that he would read at least one poem that suited his taste. But, unfortunately for him, this was not the work of an ordinary poet but rather that of a renowned Turkish communist who, in the fifties, escaped arrest and took refuge in the Soviet Union and is presently buried in Moscow. Nazım Hikmet, the most admired, revered and perhaps hated—by the Islamists-Turkish writer of the 20th century.

In the poem titled "Traitor to the Motherland" Nazım Hikmet gave voice to the plight of the less fortunate using the revolutionary dialectic of the time. Declaring that if "motherland stands for death from hunger along paved roads, if it is to shiver in the cold like dog and writhe in summer with fever, if it stands for drinking our own red blood in the factories of the bosses, if motherland is the nails of the feudal lords," than he was willing to admit that, yes he is a traitor to the Motherland!

As the police carried Ç. C. away for interrogation, his mother had a few remarkable words of her own: "Son, don't be afraid. I won't shed a single drop of tear as long as you are true to the Republic!"

How ironic that, ten days later, while visiting Washington, D.C., Recep Tayyip Erdoğan, during an interview on the program *All Things Considered*, with NPR's Robert Siegel, was reminded of the fact that five years earlier, he had been found guilty and sent to prison for reading a poem ("Minarets our bayonets...") and was asked if it was possible, today, under his regime, for someone to be arrested for reading a poem. He answered in the negative.

But I'm convinced that Kemal Atatürk had some one like Ç. C. in mind when he made his memorable address:

> O, Turkish Youth!
>
> Your first duty is to preserve and defend the Turkish independence and the Turkish Republic forever.
>
> This is the sole foundation of your existence and of your future.
>
> This foundation is your most precious treasure.
>
> In the future, too, there will be malevolent people who at home and abroad will wish to deprive you of this treasure.
>
> If, some day, you are compelled to defend the Turkish independence and Republic, do not consider the possibilities and the circumstances you may be facing! These possibilities and circumstances may prove to be extremely unfavorable.
>
> The enemies conspiring against your independence and your Republic may have won a victory unprecedented in the annals of the world. It may be that, by violence and ruse, all the fortresses of your motherland may be conquered, all its shipyards occupied, all its armies dispersed, and every corner of the country may be in fact invaded.
>
> Sadder and graver than all these circumstances, those who hold power within the country may be heedless or misguided or may even commit betrayal. Furthermore, those who hold power may identify their personal interests with the political designs of the invaders.
>
> The nation may be impoverished, ruined, and exhausted.
>
> O, the child of the Turkey of the future!
>
> Even under such circumstances, your duty is to save the Turkish independence and Republic!
>
> The strength you need is in your noble blood.

♦   ♦   ♦

How much of the predicament in which Turkey finds itself today is self-inflicted, and how much is the product of an "intelligent design" administered surreptitiously by others with vested interest in the outcome?

In *Confessions of an Economic Hit Man* (2004), John Perkins details the process by which countries have been systematically made awash in foreign debt and forced to devote an inordinate share of their national budget to paying the loans off rather than using the capital to help their dangerously impoverished citizens. In the second phase of this "operation," the creditors, working through economic hit men (EHM), bankrupt the debtor county. Ensnared, now, in a web of debt, the leaders of the country owe their political survival to the creditor nations. The final phase of the game plan consists of drawing on the leaders of the debtor nation whenever there is a need to satisfy the political, economic, or military needs of the creditors. In retrospect, the development of events during the post-1980 era looks awfully similar to the steps described by Perkins.

Let's hope that the coming days, months, and years will see Atatürk's vision of a free, independent, prosperous Turkey—a modern and contemporary civilization—becomes a reality. Let's also hope that his fear of a day when the nation calls for help does not materialize. However, current events suggest it may. The coalition of the corrupt can and will never genuinely adopt the array of political, economic, land, and administrative reforms necessary to put the country on the road to recovery. They are placing their bets on the EU, who they hope will come to the rescue, oblivious to the fact that only a country can and must save itself.

♦   ♦   ♦

Today, the enemies of Turkey are sensing that the final curtain will descend soon, perhaps sooner than one thinks, on the Kemalist play. When that happens, those responsible for its demise, the radical as well as the not-so-radical Islamists, the EU collaborationists, Karen Fogg's stable, the IMF hired hands, the advocates of surrender in the Eastern, Southeastern, Southern, and Western fronts, the enemies of the Republic, the advocates of the approaching "second Republic," those busily filling the ranks of the bureaucracy with their *imams*, the advocates of the Caliphate, and the proponents of the "nation of Islam," will all celebrate the outcome. Meanwhile, in the gilded halls of the French city of Sèvres, the EU brass will be getting ready to welcome a Turkish delegation willing to redact a new document to replace the old and antiquated one named after a Swiss town: Lausanne. The delegation, representing the country's glitterati, the "crème de la crème" of the Turkish business establishment, led by members of some of the leading families and accompanied by several retired generals and ambassadors, all vying for leadership posts in the second Republic, will affix their signatures to a new treaty, codifying the adjustments made to the borders of the Turkish Republic. They will, we will be told, recognize the Kurdish, Armenian, Cypriot, and Greek realities. In return, the EU and the USA will jointly agree to forgive Turkey's external debts to any and all EU member states and to all international institutions, such as the World Bank and the IMF. In Istanbul, Ankara and other major cities, the usual "Karen Fogg claque" of writers, will celebrate another glorious victory won by the AKP and its valiant leader against the evil forces of the enemies. Meanwhile, in a posh Paris restaurant, a couple of economic hit men will toast to a "mission" well accomplished.

◆   ◆   ◆

Nations usually learn from their past mistakes, and therefore one wishes that history will not repeat itself. Alas, that is usually just a wish. Here is how British Historian H. C. Armstrong described the scene that took place some eighty-five years ago:

> The publication of the terms of the Treaty of Sèvres had an instantaneous effect. They were, if accepted, the death sentence of Turkey. Anatolia, with Smyrna cut out, was to be supervised. Their finances were to be strictly controlled. There were to be Commissions to disband the Turkish army and control a new volunteer force and gendarmerie, to look after the taxes, the customs, the forest guards, the police. While left nominally with sovereign rights, the Turks were to be tied "hand and foot." (Grey Wolf, 1937)

And yet, history seems to repeat itself. Once again, Turkey's finances are being strictly controlled, the European Commission's commissars are ensuring that the Turkish army no longer exerts influence, taxes are being dictated by the IMF and the World Bank, and customs are being "customs-unionized"—in short, even though Turkey is nominally sovereign, Turks are being tied "hand and foot."

◆   ◆   ◆

November 12, 2005

How ironic that, as I was getting ready to depart for Europe and work on the final chapters of this manuscript, a couple of days after the nation paused and reflected, one more time, on the life and work of Mustafa Kemal Atatürk, another one of my favorite columnists, Tufan Türenç, yielded his corner to Süleyman Apaydın's poem, the very same one with which I began my journey on a hot summer day in 2004.

"Tear Down my Statues…"

What an appropriate pair to use as bookends.

The day after the Islamists' victory in the general elections of 2002, an American friend called to ask if I felt despondent and dejected, given the magnitude of the defeat of the liberal and secular forces. I told him that the future of the nation was secure as long as the true guardians of the Republic were vigilant, alert, and at their posts, just as Atatürk had charged them to be. My friend, detecting an implicit appeal to some form of extrajudicial intervention, if and when needed, questioned the appropriateness of such a move in a democratic society.

I answered him with a question: What would the judgment of history have been had the generals of the Wehrmacht, in the late 1930s, displayed courage and wisdom and intervened extrajudicially to stop a regime that had assumed power quite legally and democratically?

Even though the circumstances are vastly different and cannot be compared, I have always believed that, in the course of every historical event there comes a 'tipping point' beyond which every brave and honorable citizen must listen to the dictum of his/her conscience and do the 'right thing'.

◆   ◆   ◆

This nation has both internal and foreign enemies. Presently, the "usual suspects", after unsuccessfully trying to throw mud at the armed forces with the hope of derailing a Kemalist from assuming the position of chief of general staff, are now waiting patiently for the day when the next president of this Republic may call himself the "*imam*" of the nation. As for the external foes, their anti-Turkish attitudes are as predictable as the new moon.

Joost Lagendijk, the co-chairman of Turkey-EU Joint Parliamentary Commission, is also a good buddy of the columnist Cengiz Çandar (*Bugün*, December 29, 2005), a major crusader of the religious right, and an ardent supporter of the EU cause. (Remember Karen Fogg?) On the first anniversary of the EU vote declaring Turkey a candidate state, Lagendijk paid a visit to Turkey and immediately showed his true colors by pointing his finger at the Turkish Armed Forces as the main culprit for the terrorist plague Turkey has been fighting with for the good part of a decade. Amazing as this may sound, he implied that if only the Turkish Armed Forces would go easy on the terrorists, everything would be okay! With friends like that, Turkey doesn't need more enemies.

In this context, history ought to provide our best reference point. And the mother of all such reference points is one that is etched forever in the recesses of my mind:

> The Turks are a human cancer, a creeping agony in the flesh of the lands which they misgovern; rotting every fibre of life...I am glad that the Turk is to be called to a final account for his long record of infamy against humanity. (From a speech by British Prime Minister David Lloyd George, 1914: H. W. V. Temperley, ed., *A History of the Peace Conference of Paris*).

Dripping with hate and contemptuous, Lloyd George's speech represents the ugly side of the European attitude toward Turkey. Today, suspicion about the intentions of some EU member states continues like a ringing in the ears.

The genius of Atatürk was to rise above this hatred and vitriol and emancipate Turkey, putting it on the road to secularism and contemporary civilization and earning, in the process, the respect and admiration of old enemies. I can't think of a stronger indictment of the present Turkish regime than the juxtaposition of an Erdoğan statement—"The identity that unites Turkey is religion" (December 2005)—with the words of Ahmet Necdet Sezer, the president of the Republic:

> The designation as "Turkish Nation" of all our citizens, irrespective of their ethnic origin and religion, aims at achieving equality among citizenry and at preventing the labeling as "minority" citizens of various ethnic origins, which in fact belong to the majority. (New Year Message, January 1, 2006)

◆   ◆   ◆

Tom Brokaw called the "greatest" the generation of Americans that fought and won the battles of WWII (Tom Brokaw, *The Greatest Generation*, 1998). Anyone slightly familiar with the Turkish struggles of the War of Liberation that followed WWI will easily recognize another "greatest generation," or even two. They made the ultimate sacrifice, saved the nation from servitude, and forged a proud Republic.

What Turkey needs now is an intellectual compass that will summon all the talent and goodwill of a couple of successive generations, eager and ready to sacrifice for the common good of the nation.

But how soon will the present generation of Turks fully grasp the nature of the challenge? It's hard to tell, but I venture to say that the future of the nation will depend to a very large degree on the answer to this question. If the question is properly and clearly posed, the next generation or two will give the right answer. That they have the spiritual strength necessary for the task on hand is M. Kemal Atatürk's firm belief too:

> I have known all nations; I have studied them on the battlefield, under fire, in the face of death, when the character of a people is laid naked. I swear to you, [...] that the spiritual strength of our nation transcends that of all the world...(M. Kemal Atatürk, in conversation with H. C. Armstrong, *Grey Wolf*, 1937)

BIBLIOGRAPHY

Books in Turkish

Akçura, Yusuf. *Türkçülüğün Tarihi.* Istanbul: Kaynak, 1998.

Akpınar, Hakan. *Nasıl gazeteci oldular.* Ankara: Ümit, 2002.

Arcayürek, Cüneyt. *Sessiz Darbe.* Ankara: Bilgi, 2001.

Ateş, Toktamış. *Ne oldu bize?* Istanbul: Çınar, 1994.

Atsız, Hüseyin Nihal. *Makaleler I.* Istanbul: Irfan 1997.

Aydemir, Şevket Süreyya. *Tek Adam I, II, III.* Istanbul: Remzi, 1963.

Aydın, Erdoğan. *Nasıl Müslüman Olduk?* Istanbul: Cumhuriyet, 2002.

Boğuşlu, Mahmut. *1960–1978 Olayları, Anılar-Yorumlar.* Istanbul: 1995.

Bölük, Mehmet. *El Tayyip.* Istanbul: Toplumsal Dönü_üm, 2002.

Cemal, Hasan. *Kürtler.* Istanbul: Doğan, 2003.

Coşar, Ömer Sami. *Milli Mücadele Basını,* Istanbul: Gazeteciler Cemiyeti, 1974.

Çetin, Kaya. *Şeriat mı? Çağdaş Yaşam mı?* Istanbul: Berfin, 2004.

Çetinkaya, Hikmet. *Türkiye'nin Şeytan Üçgeni.* Istanbul: Cumhuriyet, 1998.

Denktaş, Rauf. *Rauf Denktaş'ın Hatıraları. Cilt 5-1968.* Istanbul: Boğaziçi, 1997.

Egeli, Sabahattin. *1960 Kıbrıs Cumhuriyeti Nasıl Yıkıldı.* Istanbul: Kastaş, 1991.

Erkin, Aytunç. *Fethullah Hoca'nın Şifreleri.* Istanbul: Kaynak, 2005.

Esenbel, Melih. *Ayağa Kalkan Adam Kıbrıs 1.* Ankara: Bilgi 1993.

Fırat, M. M.. *1960–71 Arası Türk Dış Politikası ve Kıbrıs*, Ankara: Siyasal, 1997.

Günsev, Mesut. *20 Temmuz 1974-Şafak Vakti Kıbrıs*. Istanbul: Kastaş, 1996.

Gürel, Şükrü S. *Tarihsel Boyut İçinde Türk-Yunan İlişkileri*. Ankara: Ümit, 1993.

Hablemitoğlu, Dr. Necip. *Köstebek*. Istanbul: Toplumsal Dönüşüm, 2003.

Ilhan, Attila (ed.)...*bir millet uyanıyor!.. v. 1*. Ankara: Bilgi, 2005.

Ilhan, Attila (ed.)/Somuncuoğlu, S....*bir millet uyanıyor!.. v. 4* Ankara: Bilgi, 2005.

Ince, Özdemir. *Mahşerin Üç Kitabı*. Istanbul: Doğan, 2005.

Kaleli, Lütfi. *Sivas Katliamı ve Şeriat*. Istanbul: Alev, 1994.

———. *Tarikat-Ticaret-Mafya-Siyaset*. Istanbul: Can, 1997.

Kışlalı, Ahmet Taner. *Ben Demokrat Değilim*. Ankara: Imge, 1999.

Küçük, Yalçın. *Isyan, v.1*. Istanbul: Ithaki Yayınları, 2005

Manisalı, Erol. *Avrupa Kıskacında Kıbrıs*. Istanbul: Derin, 2003.

———. *Türkiye-Avrupa İlişkilerinde Sessiz Darbe*. Istanbul: Derin 2003.

———. *Sömürgeleşen Türkiye*. Istanbul: Derin, 2004.

Mumcu, Uğur. *Sağcı Düşünce no. 5*. Ankara: um:ag, 1997.

———. *Orta Direk Türküleri no. 21*. Ankara: um:ag, 1997.

———. *Ermeni Mandacıları no. 23*. Ankara: um:ag, 1997.

———. *Demirel ve Çankaya no. 26*. Ankara: um:ag, 1997.

———. *Örs ve Çekiç no. 38*. Ankara: um:ag, 1997.

———. *Son Yazıları no. 40*. Ankara: um:ag, 1997.

———. *Tarikat, Siyaset, Ticaret*. Ankara: um:ag, 1988.

Mütercimler, Erol. *Kıbrıs Barış Harekatı*. Istanbul: Arba, 1990.

Özakıncı, Cengiz. *Türkiye'nin Siyasi İntiharı.* İstanbul: Otopsi, 2005.

Özol, Sezen. *Kıbrıs Barış Harekatı Günlüğü.* İstanbul: Kastaş, 2001.

Öztürk, Saygı. *Madalyalı Mahkum.* Ankara: Ümit, 2004.

Özden, Yekta Güngör. *Atatürk ve Atatürkçülük.* İstanbul: İleri 2003.

Ocak, Ahmet Yaşar. *Türk Sufiliğine Bakışlar.* İstanbul: İletişim, 1996.

Papandreu, Andreas G. *Namlunun Ucundaki Demokrasi.* Ankara: Bilgi, 1977.

Perinçek, Doğu. *Karen Fogg'un E-Postalları.* İstanbul: Kaynak, 2002.

Sadrazam, Halil. *Dr. Fazıl Küçük.* İstanbul: Kastaş, 1996.

Savaş, Vural. *Türkiye Cumhuriyeti Çökerken.* Ankara: Bilgi, 2004.

———. *Militan Atatürkçülük.* Ankara: Bilgi, 2001.

———. *Satılmışların Ekonomisi.* Ankara: Bilgi, 2002.

Soysal, Mümtaz. *Aklını Kıbrıs la Bozmak.* Ankara: Bilgi, 1995.

Sönmez, M. *Filler ve Çimenler Doğan/Anti-Doğan Savaşı.* İstanbul: İletişim, 2003.

———. *Türkiye'de Holdingler-Kırk Haramiler.* Ankara: Arkadaş, 1992.

Şener, Nedim. *Fırsatlar Ülkesinde bir Kemal Abi.* İstanbul: Güncel, 2005.

Şimşir, Bilal N. *Ermeni Meselesi 1774–2005.* Ankara: Bilgi, 2005.

———. *AB, AKP ve Kıbrıs.* Ankara: Bilgi, 2003.

Taşcı, İlhan. *Af dağının ardındaki AKP.* Ankara: Ümit, 2005.

Veziroğlu, Fuat. *Annan Planı ve Yalan Makinaları.* İstanbul: Akdeniz, 2003.

Yıldırım, Uğur. *Türkiye'de Misyonerlik.* İstanbul: Otopsi, 2005.

Yıldız, Levent Burak. *Talanya.* Ankara: Yurt, 2005.

Yusuf, H. Macit ve S. Ismail. *AB, Karen Fogg ve Kıbrıs.* Lefkoşa: Akdeniz, 2002.

Yalçın, Hasan. *Dönekler.* Istanbul: Kaynak, 2003.

Yavuz, H. ve J. L. Esposito. *Laik Devlet ve Fethullah Gülen.* Gelenek, 2004.

Yetkin, Murat. *Tezkere.* Istanbul: Remzi, 2004.

Books in English

Armstrong, H. C. *Grey Wolf.* London: Penguin, 1937.

Aslan, Reza. *No God but God.* New York: Random House, 2005.

Brokaw, Tom. *The Greatest Generation,* New York: Random House, 1998.

Cem, Ismail. *Turkey in the New Century.* Nicosia: Rustem Publishing, 2001.

Churchill, Winston. *The World Crisis: The Aftermath.* London: Butterworth, 1929.

Fleischer, Wilfred. *Sweden: The Welfare State.* New York: Greenwood, 1956.

Freely, John. *Istanbul: The Imperial City.* New York: Penguin, 1997.

Fromkin, David. *A Peace to End All Peace.* New York: Henry Holt & Co., 1989.

Goodwin, Jason. *Lords of the Horizons.* New York: Henry Holt & Co., 1998.

Gürün, Kamuran. *The Armenian File.* Nicosia: Rustem Publishing, 2001.

Heckscher, Eli F. *An Economic History of Sweden.* Harvard University Press, 1954.

Hitchens, Christopher. *Hostage to History: Cyprus.* London: Verso, 1997.

Kaplan, Robert D. *Eastward to Tartary.* New York: Random House, 2000.

———. *The Ends of the Earth.* New York: Random House, 1996.

Kinross, Lord. *The Ottoman Centuries.* New York: Morrow Quill, 1977.

———. *Atatürk-The Rebirth of a Nation.* London: Weidenfeld & Nicholson, 1964.

Kinzer, Stephen. *Crescent and Star.* New York: Farrar, 2001.

———. *All the Shah's Men.* Hoboken, NJ: John Wiley, 2003.

Köprülü, Fuad. *The Origins of the Ottoman Empire.* New York: New York State University, 1992.

Landau, Jacob M. *Pan-Turkism in Turkey.* London: C. Hurst & Co., 1981.

Macmillan, M. *Paris 1919.* New York: Random House, 2002.

Mango, Andrew. *Atatürk.* New York: Overlook Press, 2000.

———. *The Turks Today.* New York: Overlook Press, 2004.

Mastny, V. *Turkey between East and West.* Boulder, Co.: Westview Press, 1996.

McCarthy, Justin. *The Ottoman Peoples and the End of Empire.* London: Oxford University Press, 2001.

———. *Death and Exile: The Ethnic Cleansing of Ottoman Muslims, 1821–1922.* Princeton, NJ: The Darwin Press, 1995.

O Malley, B. and Ian Craig. *The Cyprus Conspiracy.* London: I. B. Tauris, 1999.

Minc, Alain. *Le Nouveau Moyen Age.* Paris: Gallimard, 1995.(in French)

Perkins, John. *Confessions of an Economic Hit Man.* San Francisco: B & T, 2004.

Pope, Nicole. *Turkey Unveiled.* New York: Overlook Press, 1998.

Sheldon, Garrett Ward. *Jefferson and Atatürk.* New York: Peter Lang, 2000.

Temperley, H. W. W. (Ed.). *A History of the Peace Conference of Paris.* Oxford: 1969.

Vonnegut, Kurt. *A Man without a Country.* New York: Seven Stories Press, 2005.

Wheatcroft, Andrew. *The Ottomans: Dissolving Images.* London: Penguin, 1993.

Periodicals in Turkish (consulted or referred to, incl. their Web sites)

Akşam	Milliyet	Stargazete	Vatan
Bugün	Ortadoğu	Tempo	Yeni Şafak
Cumhuriyet	Radikal	Tercüman	Yeniasya
Hürriyet	Referans	Türkiye	Zaman
Milli Gazete	Sabah	Vakit	

Periodicals in Foreign Languages (consulted or referred to, incl. their Web sites)

The articles *the* and *le* have not been considered in the alphabetical sequence.

Chicago Tribune	Los Angeles Times	Times (London)
Economist	Le Monde	The Wall Street Journal
Le Figaro	Middle East Quarterly	The WSJ-Europe
Financial Times	The New Anatolian	Washington Post
Foreign Affairs	The New York Times	Washington Times
Guardian	Turkish Daily News	
International Herald Tribune	Turkish Policy Quarterly	

Other Web sites (consulted and/or referred to)

www has been omitted from the addresses of all web sites

acikistihbarat.com

aksiyon.com.tr

AKParti.org.tr

atilim.org

atin.org

aydinlik.com.tr

aztagdaily.com

bilimarastirmavakfi.org

Bilgi ve Hikmet

cilicia.com

digimedya.com

deepnot.com

dorduncukuvvet.com

evrensel.net

fethullahgulen.org

gazeteciler.com

haberciler.com

habershow.com

haberx.com

haysiyet.com

herkul.org

ikincicumhuriyet.org

korkuteken.com

kurtuluscephesi.com

kuvayimedya.net

(currently shut down

by court order)

medyafaresi.com

medyakafe.com

medyatava.net

medya24.com

memleketinsesi.sinankara.com

mudafaai-hukuk.com.tr

olaymedya.com

8sutun.com

superpoligon.com

terror.gen.tr

turkishpolicy.com

yenimesaj.com.tr

INDEX

978-0-595-38716-8
0-595-38716-0